C000259216

3 Children,
3 Disabilities,
1 Family

DAVE RUSSELL

Copyright © 2018 Dave Russell

The right of Dave Russell to be identified as the author of this work has been asserted by him in accordance with the Copyright, Designs and Patents Act, 1988.

All rights reserved. No part of this publication may be reproduced, stored in a retrieval system, or transmitted, in any form or by any means, electronic, mechanical, photocopying, recording or otherwise, without the prior permission of the author.

This book is sold subject to the condition that it shall not, by way of trade or otherwise, be lent, re-sold, hired out or otherwise circulated without the author's prior consent in any form of binding or cover other than that in which it is published and without a similar condition including this condition being imposed on the subsequent purchaser.

ISBN: 978-1-99-959780-1

This book is dedicated to one person only. The person who despite everything is the central figure in which this family revolves around. She is the person who keeps this family together. The one who organises everything for everyone else. Alison Russell, without you none of us would be able to survive.

CONTENTS

ACKNOWLEDGMENTS

This book would never have happened if it was not for key people.
First off, those at Deutsche Bank who put the idea into my head after
writing articles and speaking at events over disabilities for many years.
Second is two editors who looked at this and helped me expand and
develop this piece of work.

Third is Alison, for sitting with me for hours and hours remembering
all of this and ensuring I got everything in the right order and despite
all the tears reliving this, I am eternally grateful.

Last but by no means least. My children. Anabella, Lucia and Sofia,
you are three amazing children and continue to surprise me and teach
me more each day. For everything you have gone through know that
you are forever loved, forever needed and forever special.

INTRODUCTION

I hope you find this book useful, entertaining and inspiring.

I am an autistic father of three daughters. Two of my children have very different conditions to each other and both have their own complexities. Both children need to be managed in different ways and this book will explain about their complexities.

The details explored in this book start with common issues surrounding their conditions, and my own personal experience: how I have learnt to deal with some of these issues, how I have failed, how I have had to challenge myself over an issue, and how I should treat the situation in future. I will also explore what I try to teach my girls in respect of their conditions, and how they feel when something happens. As such, there are two purposes to this book: first, to bring forward and deliver awareness with regard to disabilities and show that people who need help are no different to anyone else; and secondly, to prove to anyone like me who either has additional or complex needs, or cares for someone that has additional or complex needs, that they are amazing just the way they are. And that despite the extremely low points, it is worth it.

Over the last six years, I have been involved in employee resource groups for disabled employees. I have tried to help companies understand the huge impact and influence they have on these employees – that the help they can offer may be something small but can still have a massive impact for the employee concerned.

I have given presentations and talked about my condition and the conditions of my children at numerous events. These talks have explored various areas including caring and mental health. I have also contributed to reference material such as employee guides and flyers. I have set up informal gatherings during the day for anyone wishing to discuss or seek advice, or even just to learn a little more about a subject. I am also part of a group of people who are available for one-to-one sessions.

I think it is very important that I clarify something at this stage. I am not a doctor, psychologist or a councillor. I have not studied the conditions of my daughters in any medical depth. I am just a parent, who has struggled and still struggles to understand aspects of my daughters' conditions; a parent who must sometimes push quite hard to get help for them; a father who is constantly being surprised by his daughters, someone who is not afraid to admit that I have made mistakes and am still learning from them. Someone who is not afraid to seek advice (even if it is sometimes a little late). A father who has tried several different methods that have been suggested by professionals, fellow parents and friends, and even things I have read in self-help books. I am a father who has laughed, cried, and got frustrated. But above all, I am a father who is immensely proud of his daughters and everything they have gone through, and still go through, and I believe I am doing the best that I can do.

'It is not what you do for your children, but what you have taught them to do for themselves, that will make them successful human beings.'

'A father's "job" is not to teach his daughter to be a lady. It is to teach and show her how a lady should be treated.'

1 - WELCOME TO THE MADNESS

You don't need to be mad to work here, but it sure does help!

I laughed so hard when I first saw a poster which had this caption underneath a picture of a dog in a police helmet, in a police station, when I was about eleven. Twenty-five years later, the image and the words still make me laugh. Parenting is definitely a job of 'work' whereby, if you're sane before your first child is born, you won't be by the time your last child leaves home.

Without a doubt, parenting is one of the most difficult, underappreciated and complex jobs in the world. Additional difficulties which make the job harder arise if you are a single parent, if you yourself have additional or complex needs, or your children have additional or complex needs. You may find you have no support network around you, such as family, friends or even groups like church or school.

Before I tell you about me and the madness of my world, let me first explain certain things about perception – how parents and children are viewed, perceived and treated through the use of certain words and language. The words 'disabled' and 'special needs' sometimes make me feel that I am less than someone else. There is a stigma attached to those words; people associate them with impotence, powerlessness, incompetence and incapability. But this could not be further from the truth. I know that my children are no less than anyone else because of the conditions they have. I tend to refer to my children as having additional and complex needs. That seems to get a more proactive and engaging response than saying, 'My daughter is disabled.'

The word 'disability' tends to be linked with only physical disability. I have overheard people saying that someone does not look disabled as they come out of a disabled toilet or get into or out of a car in a disabled space. I'm sorry, I did not realise that I had to wear my special 'disability clothes' today to go and use the toilet or do my weekly shopping. Most people that I know with additional needs do not want to be viewed as different, and here's a secret: they are not any different. There is an assumption that because they have a condition they should be treated differently because of it. In part, that is correct. Someone who is in a wheelchair needs to be treated differently in terms of accessing a table at a restaurant, but not made to feel like a lesser person.

I have sometimes seen a person's face change and see that they may be thinking that they do not have the tools to manage the condition of one of my daughters. It's similar when many people think about mental health. The fact that you are suffering from a mental health disorder gives the impression that you are not sane or cannot function. The good news is that this is changing, and it is an amazing thing. Someone once said to me that the disability space is where the LGBT movement was fifteen years ago. Lots of negativity, but now being pushed into the limelight: real change is underway. It is amazing to see this change. Yes, there is still a lot to do, but it is great to see this change and to be a part of it.

My two eldest daughters are not 'disabled' at all. They do have some additional and very complex needs, as do I, but they are not any less because of it. The world is made up of lots of different people, views, languages, and it is amazing. How boring would the world be if everyone thought the same, dressed the same and lived in the same style of house. I assume that most people would not like that. Difference is what make this world an amazing place to live in. Everyone needs help at some stage, some more than others. I needed more help in English at school than I ever did with Mathematics. I was no different to any other child in my school. 'Disabilities' do not discriminate against gender, generation, race, or any other group that we have created.

Some people pass their driving test first time and others may take ten tests before passing. Does that make them a worse driver? Imagine that your insurance costs were set by how many tests you took before passing. Do you think that would be fair? Is there evidence that shows that people who pass first time have less accidents? So why should someone with autism who may need something explained to them in a different way or even a few more times than someone else be treated like they are incapable.

I am not a huge fan of social media, but it seems to me that mainly negativity is shown. Take customer reviews: there are more reviews of bad service than good. In the same way, there seems to be more bullying and insulting and mocking of disabled people than helping them or seeing the courage that they have to keep going. It is not a nice feeling, being bullied or mocked for being different. People all need help, and, sadly, if someone feels lonely or thinks that they will be mocked or bullied for speaking out, then they won't. When you were younger and needed help, you generally got it. You asked someone for help or were seen to be struggling, and you got the help you needed. It could have been as simple as help you to tie your shoelaces, or your friends helping you climb up that tree in the park. Then you become an adult and suddenly you can't get help from anyone anymore. And it seems that social media seems to glorify unpleasant behaviour. I know it is not all bad and if you search hard enough you will find people helping others, and that is great. I just wish that it would become the norm to help those who need help.

You will notice that I mentioned 'work' and 'a job' when talking about parenting. I feel that parenting is sometimes put into a box, and I think this is unfair. Parenting is not strictly a job, for many reasons. First off, you don't get paid to do it. Secondly, you don't have a line manager to check how you are doing your job (although you will have family, friends, and of course the whole social media world telling you how to be a better parent). Also, you can't quit – though sadly some people do think that they can walk away. That's a different book entirely. You are a parent, and once you become one you are a parent for the rest of your life. Even when your children grow up and have children of their own, you are still a parent. Albeit a parent with very different responsibilities to those you had before. Parenting is always evolving, and you should always try to learn and evolve with it.

So, who am I, and what is my family dynamic?

I am a father who has autism and I have three amazing young ladies. My eldest daughter, Anabella, is twelve years old; Lucia is the middle child, ten years old; and my youngest daughter is Sofia, who is seven years old. There is also a dog, Carlotta – Lottie for short. She is a year-old yellow Labrador Retriever. Along with their mum, Alison and I co-parent our children, and between us we manage all the different aspects of their care and development.

As an autistic person, I have managed over time to control and understand some of the difficulties I face. I have been able to function, to a certain degree, socially and professionally. My daughters Anabella and Lucia have two very different and complex conditions. You will see by the end of this book that the 'disabilities' that they have between them have not once held them back from doing what they want to do. Maybe some things take them longer than others, they may need to have something explained to them differently or multiple times, or instructions broken down into smaller tasks – but is that really so different to anyone else at some point or other in their lives? It has never stopped them trying anything. And most importantly, it has never stopped them succeeding.

2 - DISABILITY IN THE WORKPLACE

I mentioned previously that I have given numerous talks discussing my condition and the conditions of my daughters. I get a huge amount of pleasure from being able to stand up and speak in front of others. I found this very difficult to do earlier on in my journey, as those social skills were not very strong. I have managed to learn, through my professional career, how to interact and deliver good presentations and discussions. It also helps massively that I am extremely passionate about raising awareness for all kinds of issues surrounding disabilities and mental health. It helps that I am very open around my condition and am not ashamed or embarrassed about it or the meltdowns that do happen.

I enjoy these talks and always hope that at the end of them at least one person has gone away thinking that they are not alone and that there is support out there in various places. I also think companies are doing a lot better than previously when it comes to inclusion. Inclusion is not just about disabilities, but that is a part of it. The LGBT movement has gone through so much in the last ten to fifteen years. It is amazing to think that at some point it was illegal to be openly gay, and that now if you are gay you have the right to marry. That is amazing, and now the disability and mental health movement seems to be going the same way.

During my professional career I have worked for large FTSE 100 global banks and spoken about what it is like to be a carer. How you have to manage your personal life, your family life and your working life. All three are different and all take up lots of time: all need attention to succeed and progress. I believe that it is important that you work on each part of your life to create a balance. I have spoken many times about being a carer and how important it is to get a break. You need a break from caring to recharge. Your own mental health and wellbeing is important. If you are not well, then you are unable to look after someone else to the best of your ability.

Disability in the workplace is such a vast area that I will be unable to cover all its aspects in this chapter; however, I would like to give you an insight into some of the key things that I have experienced and that I think are important to continue this journey and keep raising awareness.

The details I give on those key aspects are based either on my own personal experience or what I have seen or been told that individuals are looking for when discussing their disability in the workplace.

Trust:

I believe that this is the most important one. Sadly, there is still discrimination around, not just in the workplace and not just against people who have additional and complex needs. As a result, people who do not have trust in the company or the management within the company will not tell them anything. This does not benefit anyone. There can be no good from this, either for the individual concerned or for the company. If the employee is struggling and requires support, it could result in the employee not being very productive or not as focused as they would be otherwise. Mistakes could be made, resulting in the need for corrections, which takes time. The employee could then be struggling twice over, as they could be worried about their workload increasing due to having to do previous work multiple times.

The company could be seeing these mistakes or performance issues and assume that the person concerned is not able to do the job. This could result in a performance review and maybe a development plan being put in place. This, in turn, would add to the employee's list of worries and struggles, as they might feel that their job was at risk. This cycle continues with no benefit to anyone.

Sadly, in my experience and speaking to others around the issue of trust, most of the time it results in the employee and company parting ways. Either the employee resigns, as they feel they have no alternative, or the company releases them. And either way, the individual's former worries are replaced with the issue of no longer having a job to support their family.

If the employee feels a level of trust towards the company or line manager, then a dialogue can be started. Ideally this will come at the point where the employee recognises the signs that they need to slow down and ask for help and support. Each person is different, and each disability presents itself in different ways. An individual may not recognise any signs that they are struggling. A line manager or colleague may notice subtle changes in behaviour or mood, which could be the early signs.

To gain the employee's trust, the company needs to have provisions in place that develop that trust. Most large companies would have a BUPA service or equivalent. This service allows an employee to have access to a trained counsellor or occupational health/therapist, which could be the first point of contact for many. Most large companies have employee resource groups which are run by employees on behalf of the employees. They are a good middle ground and would be able to direct employees to BUPA, HR or other resources that the company provides.

Communication:

Communication is as important as trust. I think the only way you can build trust is by communicating. A company should have clear communications explaining what resources are available to employees. What the process is, if you have an issue. If you are struggling, then what options are available to you.

Communication is a way to make yourself understood. It is really important because communicating is the way we express ourselves. If people do not communicate clearly with each other, there is no point communicating at all.

When communicating, you should think about the tone of your voice and your body language as well as the words you actually say. Communication is not done when you have finished speaking, but is also about listening.

As with almost anything, the more you do something, the better it becomes. Communication is no different. You have to work on your communication styles. Your body language when speaking with different audiences. How you listening to someone else. If you are a person with additional and complex needs, this may not be easy. The challenge could impact your self-confidence and therefore may end up with you feeling that you do not have the ability to communicate at work anymore, even though you have lots of important information to contribute to the discussion.

To be a really good communicator, you need to use all the tools available. One of the most important pieces in your toolkit is the ability to go at another person's pace. If someone has a stammer, then rushing the conversation is not going to help them. In fact, it will more than likely make it worse, as they will get anxious and potentially stutter more. Or worse, they will shut down and not talk, effectively stopping the discussion. Another vital tool is to follow the lead of the other person. Just as you follow their pace, you follow their lead in the conversation. This does not mean agreeing with what they say. It means allowing them to express and explain what they mean. Your job is to listen carefully and process what they are saying, and then maybe clarify points if unsure before responding appropriately.

I am not a great communicator by any stretch of the imagination. But over the last few years I have tried to improve my techniques and listen more. I have not always succeeded. Depending on the type of work you do and the environment you work in, some of these skills you will learn, practice and improve on every day. Over the last nearly fifteen years I have worked for some large global banks. Employees all over the world; lots of international colleagues whom I have had to interact with daily. A lot of them do not have English as a first language. Therefore, my communication skills had to improve so that we worked well together. Working on large global projects impact lots of different areas of a bank. I needed to understand what that impact was to different departments. I was not an expert in most areas, so I had to listen to others. I had to understand their concerns over a new process and then explain how we would resolve that concern. If neither party can communicate clearly then a project stalls and no one wins.

As a carer, I need the ability to work from home. Lucia can sometimes have seizures or get very poorly very quickly. I need to be able to work from home at short notice. I need to be able to communicate that with the company and, in turn, they need to be able to provide information on how I can work from home. What the policy is over data; what happens if I want something printed out while at home; the security on my laptop or the remote security requirements; is the remote security to connect to the company network an app that I need to install onto my phone or a physical device that I need to keep with me. This all needs to be communicated between both parties. The beauty of communication is that with technology it has become a lot easier. Maybe it can be a little more distant, losing that personal touch like a phone call or speaking face to face, but for people with anxiety it is helpful. I would log into work and send my line manager and the team an email explaining that Lucia was unwell. I would request that my work phone be diverted to my personal mobile, and then I would be working and available just like I would be in the office.

Language:

Communication is key, but equally important is the language that you use while communicating. Language is something that I was never really any good at. I was always good with numbers, but not so much with words. I would generally use the same word to cover a range of situations, like 'speak' for example. I would not use the word 'talk' or 'say' or 'whisper' or 'shout'. A person speaks, but the use of the word 'shout' implies something else. Why are they being loud? Are they shouting for help? Are they shouting because they are somewhere noisy? Could they not like the other person and are therefore shouting at them in anger? Very different from a whisper, which could imply closeness between the two people talking.

I attended a legal working group in 2018 and a guy spoke about communication and language being the biggest thing to help people, and he said that the choice of vocabulary makes a big difference. I was not sure what he meant at the time – as I said, I am more numbers than words. The example he gave was 'reasonable adjustments'. This was part of the Disability Act, now called the Equality Act, 2010. A workplace must make reasonable adjustments to ensure that a person with a disability is not disadvantaged and that steps are taken to remove, reduce or prevent obstacles that they may face while doing their job.

The UK government changed the wording from 'disability discrimination' in 2005. But what is a 'reasonable' adjustment? It differs for each person and is based on their needs. For example, someone in a wheelchair will potentially needs an adjustable desk or a lower desk to work on. And wider doors to ensure that a wheelchair can pass through easily. For someone who suffers from high levels of anxiety or has a fear around large crowds of people, requesting that they start work earlier and leave earlier is an option. I know some autistic colleagues who start at 8 a.m. in the City and finish at 4 p.m. to avoid the crowds, as they can get very anxious around large groups of people.

Would you say that either of these adjustments is unreasonable? I do not think so. I would suggest that they are sensible, and in today's global business environment a person moving an hour sideways from the usual nine-to-five has minimal impact on the business. If it did, then I would say that there was a failure within the business set-up.

Therefore, the speaker said, we should change 'reasonable' to 'workplace' adjustments. The idea behind this is that the word 'reasonable' implies that you are asking for something 'unreasonable'. This is not the case in most requests. The example given was that a person using a wheelchair is not being 'unreasonable' when asking that doors are wide enough to allow a wheelchair access. This example stuck with me, and I decided to look at the language that I use. I have since tried to change how I use the English language.

The first time an editor reviewed this book, she commented on my use of language. How I came across, and what I was trying to explain in these pages. She fully understood what I was trying to get across, but the tone of my words was not helpful to the reader. As I said, I tend to use one word for an action in every context, but I shouldn't. Each context is different, each conversation you have is different. Each person you speak to has a different approach and communicating style, and the best thing to do is to tailor your style and use of language to the situation. In order to do this, you need to learn about the use of language and how it impacts others.

3 - DIAGNOSIS

Anabella was born in May 2006 and has been diagnosed with moderately severe ASD (autism) and ADHD. ASD stands for Autistic Spectrum Disorder. ADHD is Attention Deficit Hyperactive Disorder. This diagnosis was completed in April 2016. In total it took ten years to get Anabella formally diagnosed. As parents, we first suspected something with Anabella when she was around three to four years old. That was the start of a six-year battle. During those six years, we had to battle with her school, doctors, specialists and other health professionals. Six years, in my opinion, is too long for this sort of diagnosis.

The hardest challenge and the biggest battle we had was with the school. The reason being, the school provides their report and opinions to the health professionals, who would consider the school's opinion over the parents' – especially, in my experience, if the child in question is their first child. The schools have a very hard job. That job has not been made any easier over the last decade by funding cuts and constant changes to the curriculum, etc. The health service is always struggling as well. It is not easy for them either. The difficulty I and other parents in similar situations have found, is that once a healthcare professional gets told by the school that the child is fine, or that it is a phase, it is very difficult to be taken seriously. As a parent you get put into the 'over-reacting' category; or worse, the 'neurotic' group. Neither is very helpful.

I do believe that this was one of the key issues we had. As the school believed it was a phase (although they acknowledged her social skills were behind her peer group), they were not worried, and said she would catch up in time. This meant that no interventions were done. No analysis of her behaviour to see any patterns. No sessions set up to improve and develop her social skills. In the case of Anabella there were two key areas in which I feel we were given no help. Because her social skills and her literal understanding of things was not as developed as her peers, she could be inappropriate, and as a result was bullied and also got the reputation of a troublemaker. By extension: if a teacher sees a child as a troublemaker, that reputation is difficult to change, but not impossible. However, if the headteacher also believes that this is the case, then you have a near impossible task of getting any support from the school.

As parents, we discussed the situation with the school, and mainly with her class teacher. Most of the staff went through the motions and did not really do anything to help Anabella or give us the support to get her the help she needed. We did, however, get a breakthrough with one teacher when discussing her attention levels. She agreed that she could have some high-calorie biscuits after lunch to hopefully help her concentration in class. This actually started working after a few weeks. Not brilliant, but a start. However, it sadly did not last very long. Teachers need support as well and they get support from LSAs (Learning Support Assistants). Unfortunately, Anabella's LSAs thought that she should not be eating food in class and therefore moved her outside the classroom into a 'pod' area – the area used when a child needs a timeout. Anabella then thought that she was in trouble; she got anxious and therefore started taken longer and longer to eat her biscuits. In the end the LSAs decided that she was being silly and therefore rushed her, and so, in the end, she only ate one of them or sometimes only half, instead of the two that we agreed with her teacher.

Sadly, that enlightened teacher left at the end of the year. Anabella was in year four at the time, and her reputation was made worse because now the assistants believed that she was messing around.

We finally managed to make headway when the headteacher moved on to another school. A new headteacher came in, unaware of Anabella's reputation. Of course, there was the risk that they would listen to the teachers already there. But at least there was a chance for someone to look at the situation with a fresh set of eyes.

In the end, we were correct. We discussed the issues with Anabella, the bullying, the help we were trying to get. We were honest and agreed that Anabella was not the easiest child and sometimes did put herself in those situations. And this was why we needed to get support for her. The new head was positive and agreed to review and see what we could do.

At this point, Lucia had been born. She was already diagnosed with 22q11 deletion syndrome and had had a few operations. I believe that it was because of everything we had gone through as parents with Lucia that we were then removed from the 'over-reacting and neurotic' category. We were taken seriously and given support from the new headteacher.

It is important to ensure that you are getting support from your school if you are looking to get a diagnosis and support from healthcare professionals. The one thing we did not do as much as we should have done as parents was fight harder. We went through the motions to some extent and kept trying to be nice to the school, not wanting to upset everyone. Well, the process has taught me one thing: do not worry about upsetting the school. Neither the teachers, the head, nor even other parents. The reality is that your child will be at school for five years or so. When your child leaves, the school will move on and not worry about the support your child may still require. You may then have difficulty in secondary school: the battle for support must start again at a school that might not think that whatever issues your child has are serious, because nothing came from the primary school.

With Lucia, we make sure that we keep a closer eye on things than we did with Anabella. If I have to go into the school every week for an update, then I will do. Do not give up, it is certainly is not easy. It is your child, it is their future and their education, so you need to fight for every inch of support you can get.

Lucia was born in April 2008 and has been diagnosed with 22q11 deletion, also known as DiGeorge syndrome. This diagnosis was completed in August 2008 after identifying a heart murmur. For Lucia, we still had a little battle with some health professionals to take us seriously. This time, the health professionals kept saying that Lucia was fine, just on the lowest percentile regarding her weight and milk intake. But since the diagnosis, the support has been amazing.

The first issue was with the monitoring of the baby. As Lucia was our second child, they just went through the motions, I think. Not a full scan, just the tests that they thought necessary, and they were not alarmed when Alison was huge with Lucia very early. Alison is only five foot one. When she is pregnant, she has a large belly and can look larger due to her small height. They did not seem alarmed during the pregnancy. However, upon delivery, the midwife was very alarmed because Lucia was very tiny. Most of it was water. The doctor advised when she was diagnosed that this is common: the more water, the greater chance of something not being quite right.

The bigger issues came soon after. Lucia was consistently tired; she slept a lot, more than a new-born baby usually does. When we gave her milk, she did not drink a lot. At first, it was thought that it was the milk. We changed the milk and monitored her intake. No difference. We spoke to the health visitor and was told that although she was on the lowest percentile, she was still in range, and therefore no worries.

That is not helpful information when you feed your child and she falls asleep after only one ounce of milk, which is not enough. I have been told that babies do not sweat, as the sweat glands have not developed yet. However, when Lucia was sucking on a bottle of milk she was working really hard and her head was wet and clammy. At the time I thought it was sweat, but the actual reason was the hole in her heart, which had to work twice as hard as normal, which made her tired. It was because of all this sleeping and lack of milk intake that we decided that we would stop going to the health visitor and midwife support team and go straight to a doctor. Alison took Lucia to our local doctor, and within five minutes she called the paediatrician at our local hospital and told them that Lucia needed to be seen today.

Alison took her in, and within twenty minutes of seeing a doctor he had found a murmer in her heart, and admitted her. He also suspected that she had 22q11 deletion syndrome, given with her physical appearance. He performed the tests and it was confirmed.

Sofia was born in October 2010 and so far, aside from the usual seven-year-old's fights with her elder siblings and pushing boundaries, she is perfectly fine – just slightly crazy. Remember her name, as she will either rule the world or destroy the world. So, either

Prime Minister or Lex Luthor … It will be exciting to see how this ends.

It is important to realise that all children are different and that disorders and conditions develop over time. Some are genetic, and others are a result of the environment around us. Sofia understands that her sisters are different and require different things. She is aware of the medicine that Anabella takes and the support equipment that Lucia needs to wear and how it impacts her. Equally, she does what every younger child does: she wants to do the same things as her elder sisters. She wants to play with them, she wants to learn and have fun. We do not stop any of our children learning and playing with each other, despite their conditions and the restrictions they have. They just find a way to not let it stop them doing what they want to do.

Why is diagnosis important?
In summary, if you are not diagnosed then you cannot get any help. I think it is extremely difficult, especially currently, to get help if a health professional does not agree with your instincts. Help is something that everyone needs at some point, and it can take away the perception of a naughty child or a defensive adult.

In the case of the autism and ADHD, the right help allows the person and everyone around them – family, friends, partners, employers, colleagues and teachers – to understand why they react the way they do to certain things. Why they may experience difficulties, and how to overcome them.

Lucia's diagnosis was important in terms of understanding why she was sleeping for longer periods of time that she should be. She was only awake for a maximum of two hours a day. We now knew why she was unable to take any milk and fell asleep constantly during a feed. The diagnosis, I believe, saved my daughter's life as it allowed her heart defect to be identified and repaired before the pressure placed upon her heart stopped it completely, which was a possibility.

How is autism diagnosed?
In the UK a diagnosis is done by a multi-disciplinary team that consists of a paediatrician, a speech and language therapist, a psychiatrist and maybe a psychologist.

The characteristics of autism vary from one person to another, although a diagnosis would look at a person having persistent difficulty with social communication and interaction, and restricted and repetitive patterns of behaviour, activities or interests since early childhood. These are assessed to see if they limit or impair everyday functioning.

A lot of parents I have spoken with were extremely worried about having their child 'labelled' with autism. I would say the same thing now as I said to them then. So what? The label that you are so worried about allows them and you to get help. If ignorant people wish to label a child, I hate to say it but they already have labelled the child – normally as a troublemaker. Anabella was classed as a troublemaker before the diagnosis by certain members of her primary school. This remained the case with some even after the diagnosis, as they refused to believe it. It makes it very hard for someone who needs help to get that help when people keep believing that they know best, based on nothing other than their own opinion. It is best to always keep an open mind. Easier said than done, I know, but it's worth spending some time understanding why, for example, a child keeps throwing a tantrum when you take them onto the grass; it may not be that they do not like sports. It may be that the texture of the grass makes them extremely anxious. I know a child who cannot go on the grass for this reason: the texture makes them very anxious and can result in them shouting and running off the grass.

Now Anabella is at secondary school. The school was made aware of her condition from the first day and have support in place for her. She has decided to only tell a few friends that she is autistic, and this is her choice. She explained that these friends now understand a little better when she says something which could come across as hurtful or inappropriate.

How is ADHD diagnosed?
ADHD is diagnosed in a similar way to autism, in terms of a team establishing that your behaviour impacts everyday functioning and that the behaviour is not a symptom of an underlying mental health condition. Diagnosing ADHD in adults is harder than with children. The medical profession is conflicted as to which symptoms apply and should those same symptoms be relevant for both adults and children. Currently the process in the UK must show a direct link with childhood. Symptoms must have been present from childhood

to now.

In short, if the symptoms have not been present from your childhood into adulthood, you will not be diagnosed with ADHD because it is believed that ADHD cannot develop for the first time in an adult.

Well, people once 'believed' that the world was flat and now we know that the world is round. I do not know if ADHD can develop in an adult if not present in the child, but the question someone should be asking is how does ADHD develop? Once we have understood this, we will know if it can develop in an adult. I think at the moment we are making assumptions based on an absence of proof.

How is 22q11 deletion syndrome diagnosed?
Considering how complex this condition is, it is extremely simple to check and diagnosis someone. A simple blood test, no assessments or reviews. No multi-team of professional experts discussing your history and symptoms. Just some blood and a specific analysis of that blood. It can also be done if you are pregnant by testing the pregnancy fluid, similar to how a child is tested for Down's syndrome.

So the test is very simple and relatively painless and not invasive. Why is this test not done regularly? The fact is, 22q11 deletion syndrome is not a common condition. It is also not one of the conditions that are tested for unless you have the condition and are pregnant – when the chances of passing it on are 50%. The NHS cannot test for every single condition on every child born, so that is understandable. The good news is that there are some physical traits which could indicate that someone has this condition and therefore warrant this type of blood test, which is how Lucia was diagnosed.

4 – AUTISM

What is autism, or ASD?

Well, you could google it and find articles on the subject from all over the world. There are several charities and organisations that provide support, advice and even research into the causes of autism. I have taken some of the most common issues that have been identified, and ones which I experience myself or with Anabella.

First off – I can tell you what autism isn't. It is not an illness or disease and it is not something that goes away. It is a condition which has no cure currently. Autism is a disorder that you are either born with or is present very early on in the development stage. Put simplistically, it affects human behaviour – essential behaviours such as social interaction, communication (ranging from ideas, feelings and the imagination) – and establishing relationships. It also affects how you perceive the world. It is a disorder which has a massive range (hence the 'spectrum'). It has life-long effects. You do not 'grow out of it', although some symptoms or aspects of autism may vary over time.

Autism sometimes presents mental health issues, when a person feels upset, worried or even scared. Depression is quite common with autistic people, and I can tell you depression is a hard thing to survive aside from any other condition, making a complex battle within yourself even more complicated.

There are some strong and consistent commonalities within the spectrum, especially in social deficits, which are used to test and confirm a diagnosis.

What are some of these characteristics?

- Sensory issues
- Mental functionality
- Seizures
- Communication difficulties
- Disruptive behaviour

This is not an exhaustive list by any means, but some characteristics I have witnessed in children on the spectrum, including my daughter, and in myself in varying degrees.

An autistic person sees, hears and feels the world differently to others. Often people feel that being autistic is a fundamental aspect of their identity. I personally have no issues with being autistic and am happy to explain to others that I am. Some aspects of my autistic behaviour are subtle, and others more extreme. It all depends on the situation. For example, I exhibit a lack of eye contact, or at least very limited eye contact, during an interview. It is something that I feel now is best declared beforehand, as I have had feedback that the interviewer can feel that I am not interested in the role or not confident enough to answer the questions. This is not the case, and in fact it is actually the opposite for me: the more I tend to look around the room, the more I am processing the situation. No point telling them after the interview – the damage is already done at that point. Not everyone is as comfortable as me, though, and I can understand why some people do not declare it. I would like to think that declaring it will mean that the interviewer will have an open mind and will listen to my words as opposed to focusing on my behaviour. Sadly, I know that this is often not the case, and that they use my condition as a reason not to progress me.

The reasons for this I cannot explain. If I were to speculate, I would say it is because they are nervous about doing any workplace adjustments that they may need to do to enable me to work at my best. A lot of workplace adjustments for me would be no different for anyone else without autism. I prefer to come in early and I find it easier to work in a corner away from others, or in a position where I cannot disturb others. The reason is that I walk around, especially when on the phone. If I am trying to resolve data issues I will walk around and tend to get in other people's way. So this adjustment benefits others as well as me.

I know that it is illegal to use a disability as a reason to not hire someone, but in practice it is done. It makes it very difficult for people to be honest and open. Even more so now, when there are so many job losses. Everyone is fighting to keep their jobs or to get a job – the last thing you want to do is give someone an excuse.

How common is autism?
Good question – I know that when I was growing up, autism was not very common. However, I believe that this was due to the amount of people being diagnosed and the condition being less generally known. There is now more disclosure and/or diagnosis than before, although maybe not as much as there should be. It is understandable why it is not always disclosed, as I can speak from personal experience of losing a job because of being autistic.

The figures I have provided below are based on surveys and estimates from 2011. I was unable to find anything more recent, but if there are more recent verified statistics, please let me know, as it would be great to see how the trend is going.

- World population: 1%
- US population: 1 out of 68 and therefore 3.5m
- UK population: 1% adult population – therefore around 700,000

When I was researching to see how common autism was, I was surprised that it was more common than I originally thought. Thinking back about awareness and when disabilities were discussed at school and with friends, I remember it being minimal at best. The increase could be a mixture of a better understanding of the condition and better ways to identify children and adults who are autistic. Autism is a very difficult condition because one of the key issues is social behaviour. Social skills and behaviour are very hard for an autistic person, so it is very easy to annoy or frustrate someone else. Also, a lot of research spoke about 'socially acceptable' behaviour. Again, this is very subjective. People are different and so is each person's behaviour and tolerance. We need to raise awareness for autism and other conditions, to try and get others to have a higher level of tolerance. Personally, I feel that society needs more tolerance of anyone who is different; that includes anyone who does not have a disability. It seems that if you disagree with someone's point of view or opinion then you get told you are stupid or get abused. You only need to look at social media to see someone commenting on someone else's life choice, and then, sadly, a few comments later it ends up turning abusive. With this kind of behaviour rife, you can see why many people with a disability choose not to disclose it. Now, this maybe largely due to social media: it is always easier to comment on something when you are on the other side of the world and cannot be confronted in person about your views. Someone said to me that you hear more negative feedback/reviews than positive, and I would like to think that the balance of people's views on disabilities is the same. You see and hear more of the unacceptable behaviour and abuse, but in fact it is a small minority. However, if this is all we see, then sadly someone with autism could believe that it is what most people believe.

How do autistic people perceive the world?
This one is a very hard question to answer. I have read a lot to see how others see the world and their place in it. I can explain and explore how I see the world, but that would not help you understand some of the key things that an autistic person can feel generally. Again, this is entirely subjective, but I would encourage you to understand that if one autistic person feels something, then others may do so as well. There is no harm in assuming that the next autistic person you meet (or even the next person full stop, regardless of any additional or complex need they may or may not have) may see the world differently to you. The reality is that they probably will see one aspect of the world differently to you; it could be religion, social values, family values, or which is the best sport. It will be a different view, and that is the beautiful thing about our world. So many differences to learn from; so many different experiences to share. What would you learn from someone who believes and acts exactly as you do? Nothing that you do not already know.

Some autistic people say that they feel very overwhelmed when they are out, and it causes considerable anxiety, especially when it comes to understanding and creating relationships with other people.

I still come across people I do not always understand, and I have very few relationships with people. I have ended up losing relationships due to misunderstanding how someone reacted, what they said, how I thought they looked. I have even lost relationships over how they did not react which I misunderstood.

Taking part in normal everyday activities such as family interactions, school, work and general social life can be very hard for some autistic people, adults and children alike. Some autistic people know how to interact and communicate with others; others struggle to build a rapport with people. This includes other autistic people. I have managed to improve dramatically my interactions with people and build an initial rapport through work and managing certain situations, but there are still varying degrees of anxiety, depending on the context.

Why am I different?
This is something I asked myself for years before my diagnosis, and something that I am now extremely proud of. I embrace the fact that I am different to others, in how I read situations, how my brain works and sees things – the fact that, for example, when I am anxious I will pretend to play an imaginary piano while sitting in a restaurant. I am not ashamed of it and do not feel like I have to hide my little 'quirks', but I do understand that sometimes, depending on the situation, a different strategy may be needed. One thing I find difficult to explain is, if I am anxious and playing an imaginary piano in the restaurant, why others look at me and either laugh or frown. I feel bad. Not because of what I am doing, but more because I feel like I am ruining their evening. Again, this depends on the situation and how I am feeling at the time. Another example is when I am at work: I walk around my desk when I am on the phone and explaining something, and if I feel that someone does not understand what I am trying to get across, then I can get frustrated. I can see something very clearly in my mind and it makes perfect sense, so I do not understand why others cannot see it. It does not help that I am unable to explain clearly what I see. I will walk around with a headset on the call, and I will clap or wiggle my fingers while talking. I would not clap my hands in the theatre if I was feeling anxious, as it would disturb others, so I will maybe play the piano on my leg or just wiggle my fingers or hold a friend's hand. Something subtle, for the

environment I am in. Sometimes, however, it is not always possible; it depends on the level of anxiety I am experiencing.

A lot of autistic people feel very different to others and some believe that people do not understand them, including friends and family. Anabella has said to me on numerous occasions that she feels different and that no one understands her, including me.

One of the key things, which is the biggest barrier in my opinion, is that autism is a non-physical disorder. By that, I mean that you cannot 'see' the issue: I do not 'look' disabled. When Anabella is anxious and therefore maybe clapping or jumping up and down, the automatic thought of most people is that she is being naughty. And I am a bad parent, as I let my child get away with that behaviour. Maybe I should start a side business designing 'disabled clothing' because it seems that everyone but me knows how a disabled person should look.

Anabella and I were in Lakeside one weekend – I think we were going to buy a present for her as she had earned some stickers: her behaviour had been very good for a month or so. We were walking to get some hot chocolate and there was a large group of teenagers who just been to the cinema, laughing and having fun. They just appeared, and we were very close, so it was a bit of a shock for Anabella, very loud.

Anabella and I both have sensory issues. Some things seem louder to us than they actually are – I have seen it classed as 'over-sensitive hearing'. So to us the teenagers' noise was like screaming and shouting, and Anabella thought that they were all angry and upset with each other, and got scared. I could tell it was not that, that is was fun, but it was still loud even for me.

Anabella started to get very anxious. She grabbed my pocket and froze and started to cover her ears. She also started looking around trying to find somewhere to go to get away from the noise. She then started to head to the nearest store, but she was not paying attention to her surroundings and therefore bumped into a few people walking nearby. I tried to get control of her, as she would just run away if I was not careful. If someone was in her way she would not really see them and would take a direct route to get away, meaning going straight through them. She would see where she needed to go and just head straight for it, regardless of any obstacles.

The group were heading towards us and there was nowhere really to go. I took Anabella to one side and then on my knees tried to settle her by telling her she was safe at the side with me and that they were having fun, so it was all okay. Some of the group realised that she was anxious because of them. Some of them stopped talking or lowered they volume; others did not notice; and some of them laughed. Well, that was fine. Teenagers are still learning and developing and finding out about themselves. Adults you would think know better. But the reality is, an adult is still learning too. If they are not informed about something, they will draw their own conclusions. One thing that happens a lot more than it should is an adult walking by with their child and then pointing at Anabella and telling their own child that she is a very naughty child; that her behaviour is unacceptable and that they should never behave like that. I do not think this is productive for anyone. It could result in the child of that parent keeping all their feelings in rather than expressing their emotions or anxiety. This has nothing to do with having a disability or not. Anabella gets worse if an adult is pointing at her and saying that she is unruly. She retreats into her shell further, and does not express her concerns. Neither helps raise awareness in others and creates a tolerant society in which people can be who they are.

Yes, I can see how it looks from the outside as well: a child showing massive signs of disruptive behaviour in a public place is hard to ignore. However, from the outside, people do not know what is going on. It is very easy to make assumptions, and everyone does it, including me. Commenting negatively on the basis of those assumptions makes the situation harder. I do not expect people to understand what is going on with Anabella when she has a meltdown – or with me when I am anxious – but it would be nice if people didn't make snap judgements.

Adults who are autistic often feel that they are misunderstood. Not a big surprise when you look how people communicate. Dr. Albert Mehrabian conducted several studies on non-verbal communications and he deduced that 7% of a message is conveyed through the actual words, 38% through vocal elements, and the remaining 55% through non-verbal elements (such as facial expressions, gestures, posture, etc.). An autistic person who is very literal – unable to understand the majority of someone's body language and recognise differences in the pitch of a voice and what that means – only understands 7% of what is said. And because of the lack of non-verbal clues, they may even misread that 7%. This is very important to understand when speaking to an autistic person.

I cannot tell you the number of messages I have misunderstood from friends and family over social media or on a mobile phone because of my literal reading of a situation. My responses then create a further series of reactions, which end up confusing me even more. I have sadly lost several friendships due to this, and some of my friendships are now very different to how they were before. Now I try to give my interpretation of things which I am not 100% sure of, to try and mitigate any misunderstanding. I have even told people that I think I have misunderstood something, and then explained, and still got reactions which could and have ended friendships or relationships.

This is not just a function of the magic of WhatsApp and other social media apps; it has also happened in my professional career, through emails with senior stakeholders or my peers and colleagues.

I have come to believe that social media has been amazing in one way: our ability to reach so many people around the world, to interact with them and share special moments with others who may be on the other side of the world. That is fantastic. I have a small group of friends around the world, and to share things with them when they are so far away is really special. It has been reported by healthcare professionals that social media is like a drug. You get all happy when a photo on Instagram or Facebook gets a 'like' – when people comment and like the latest status you have posted. Sadly, it works the other way around too. People will make comments because they did not like a photo, or a 'friend' who is no longer a friend makes a comment about something private, which then gets everyone involved. Next time you go to a restaurant or pub or any social gathering, see how many people within a group are on their phone. It will be a lot, in my experience. I have been out with a team of fifteen and at least ten of them were on their phone, looking at Facebook or messaging someone when we were meant to be having a bonding session.

Schools are now looking at introducing non-mobile days to encourage social interaction, as many young people do not have those skills at an age when the older generation did. Maybe I am being dramatic. Normally the worst-case scenarios are hyped up and exaggerated to make a point. I do not see the day when people will sit across from each other and have an interview by WhatsApp, so I think we are safe (although that would make a good comedy sketch!).

5 – AUTISM CHARACTERISTICS

Sensory Issues:

Many articles and websites state that a large number of children with autism are highly aware of, or can be extremely sensitive to, certain sounds, textures, tastes and smells. This can also extend to light, colours, temperature and even pain. There seem to be two types of sensitivity, either an over- or an under-sensitivity. I can relate to this, both personally and with Anabella. There are certain things that you would not think could generate the reaction of a child dropping to the floor and screaming: things like turning a vacuum cleaner on, or a telephone ringing, or even the feel of a jumper on their bare skin. These are reactions to everyday things that you can only deal with if you know what is going behind the scenes.

For those of you who have no experience with ASD, believe me when I tell you that this is not an overreaction. This is perfectly normal for people with the condition, and the feelings they are experiencing are real. I personally hate wearing a coat, for example, regardless of the weather; I would rather get soaked, as I often get extremely hot and feel trapped, which results in a highly agitated state whereby I clap my hands, play the imaginary piano with my fingers. The strange part is that I am known to always have a coat attached to my bag, although very rarely wear it.

So why do I even take one out? Good question. To which the

answer is simple: as a child I was taught to always take a coat when was is cold or raining, so I now do it all the time. I just cannot wear it for long, that's all. I take a lot of things very literally, especially instructions, and I have a very long memory when it comes to those instructions.

This gives you a little insight into how an autistic person puts things together. One of the biggest difficulties that I have is explaining why I do things. The reason being is that these are normal behaviours for me, so it is like trying to explain why the traffic lights have red at the top. They just do. It has always been like that, and trying to explain it is difficult. Sometimes you just have to accept what you are told at face value.

Why does this happen?
The reaction of one person to another is based on how your brain interprets the signals received. Some children do not seem to notice extreme cold, or pain. One child with autism may fall and break their arm and not even cry, yet another child may scream with alarm because someone has held their hand.

Anabella does not do very well if you try to hold her hand, she never has. She tends to hold onto my bag if I have one, or the pocket of my hoodie or jeans. She always used to stand on the left or she gets anxious and disruptive. This was because, during road-safety week at primary school, she was told children should be on the left, so they are furthest away from the road while walking on the pavement. Nowadays she manages to be on either side without undue concern. She is growing up and therefore needs to be able to make her own decisions. When she was little it was not feasible to have her not holding my hand while crossing the road. I had to have control of her, as she did and still does have a dangerous habit of walking off when anxious. While crossing a road, she would walk or even run off.

When Anabella was little, I could pick her up and cross the road, although she fought a little as she wanted to walk and be a big girl. But part of being a good parent is recognising when to release them a little more.

There have been dangerous moments, however. When I tried to let her cross next to me but not holding hands, she would notice something, a can on the road, a door being opened in a car park, or even someone looking at their phone and the screen's light coming on, and she would run towards it. She was seven years old at this stage. I had to grab her to stop her running into oncoming traffic. Try to hold her hand and it would start again: she would pull away from me, not sensing the dangers of our surroundings.

Due to this, and the fact of having three young children, I tend to get to shopping centres like Lakeside very early so that there are not too many people (I don't like too many people around) and Anabella has a little licence to walk around freely. She never goes far, is always close to hand, but she gets a little freedom, and this makes the day better.

One day we were shopping and as it started to get busier she got closer and closer to me, which was excellent as I didn't have to physically bring her close (normally I do). She started grabbing my jacket pocket, which made me extremely anxious myself as I do not like being touched and this felt like pulling. I took her hands off me and she did it again and again, and this went on for a while. She then grabbed one of the bags I was holding and that was fine for both of us. After that shopping trip, I thought about her behaviour. Anabella did what she did to make herself feel safe.

For weeks this happened, and sadly no compromise could be found with the pocket-holding, but I realised how important it was for Anabella. She would do it crossing a road too, and she was so much calmer then. It was at this point that I realised I needed to do something to calm myself down about the pocket, not get Anabella to change her behaviour. She had managed to find a way to keep her safe and close to me. This was what I wanted, this was what I was teaching her. It was more important for me to change my behaviour than it was to teach Anabella to hold my hand for my benefit. The holding of the pocket was very difficult at the beginning, but weeks of wearing a hoodie indoors with Anabella holding my pocket while we watched a film seemed to help a great deal. Eventually, this was one of her ways she used to calm herself down and walk sensibly when we went out.

Now she no longer needs to hold my pocket, although there is the odd day where she will grab my bag or pocket. In turn, there are days with me as well when for whatever reason I will become anxious, but Anabella and I communicate and work something out that benefits us both. Normally my anxiety arises for a different reason, not because of her holding my bag or pocket.

Anabella has also learnt to hold my hand. She doesn't do it for long, and normally I am the only adult whose hand she will hold. She will also hold her sisters' hands but not another child's, so when school trips took place and she had a partner and was told to hold hands it never went well. Still, the school enforced it, and then wondered why they got disruptive behaviour for the whole trip. The school was made aware of the hand-holding issue, but still chose to enforce the rule rather than try any of the alternatives suggested. As a result, we were informed that Anabella might not be able to go on any more trips outside of the school as it was unsafe for her.

What works with one child may not work with another. That is one of the reasons we are taught different methods of problem-solving in mathematics. There is nothing wrong with that. How I work out a problem at work may be different to someone else. As long as you are both working towards your objective and get the right results, then it does not matter how you do it.

What next?

The situation with Anabella not holding hands could have continued until she was old enough to not hold hands. It would have worked itself out – but at what cost? We would have been unable to do shopping trips; we would have run the risk of her getting run over in a car park; she would have been excluded from activities 'just in case'. That would not be fair to her sisters, her parents, or her. It is not her fault that she does not like holding hands. You don't force an adult to eat carrots if they do not like them; why force a child to do something that clearly causes distress just because those are 'the rules'?

Anabella knew what she needed – I didn't, but she did. She couldn't explain at first why holding my hand caused so much anxiety. But I decided to trust my daughter and see what would happen, and she found a way to feel safe and to allow me to feel safe with her. She obviously knew that I wanted her near me at certain times but couldn't understand why holding my hand was important. Especially as she couldn't do it for long, if at all.

I made the mistake of trying to enforce what I was taught as the only way to have control in a situation that warranted holding her hand. It worked for us, so should work for our children. But I was taught by my daughter a better way for her. It took longer than it should have, and I should have been more open-minded, but no child comes with an instruction manual, and even if she had, I wouldn't have read it anyway. Very few men ever do.

Mental functionality:

Many people with autism have some form of mental dysfunction. As this is a spectrum, you can have some variation, ranging from the extreme to the minor. Some areas may be normal and other areas will be weak. For example, a child may do really well in a test that measures visual skills, but be extremely weak in an area using language.

This is a very difficult thing to understand, in my opinion. I struggle with it when, for example, Anabella explains that she does not understand something from school that day. I try and explain it in a different way, but sometimes after trying maybe three or four different ways to explain, she still doesn't fully understand. How do I help her? How do I know which way works best for her? What if it is not the way I am explaining it but the subject matter? All these things could have an impact, or none of them. It is also difficult for Anabella to explain to me what it is that she finds helpful.

I myself find it very frustrating if I do not understand something and the more someone explains and I still do not understand, the more anxious and frustrated I get, and so end up walking away. Or perhaps I have picked up on a certain word and taken it literally, and then am unable to move on from the subject until the word is explained. Maybe I have misunderstood the context of a certain word that could change the entire direction of the conversation. It is better to just leave the subject and come back to it another day.

I try not to get into too much detail if I have misunderstood something or do not understand something. I will ask, maybe twice, and after that I'll switch off. It is not because I do not care or think another opinion is invalid (although it can come across like this at home and in meetings with work): it is my way of ensuring that I do not get too anxious or become disruptive. Sometimes I have found that just sitting back and listening gives me more information to process and then a certain word that I did not understand makes more sense. I also remember a quote from Teresa from the television series Sharpe saying that God gave you two ears and one mouth. In other words, you should listen twice as much as you speak. It is not always easy, and I still mess up, but I have realised that I am less anxious and more productive when I listen more.

I have found that it is best to not push too hard with Anabella when she does not understand (although I still make the mistake of doing it sometimes – and I'm sure Anabella will say that I do it more than sometimes, if she is ever asked), and give her time to work it out herself. Sometimes she does, and other times she doesn't. Sometimes she finds a pattern in something and works it out and I worry about whether that pattern will work with other questions or situations. At the end of the day, if she has the tools to work problems out then that's good. Life is about problem-solving, and you do not always use the same tool for each problem. You can only do what you can, based on the tools and information you have in front of you at the time.

Seizures:

As many as a quarter of children with autism will develop seizures. One in four children could be subject to seizures from early childhood or as they become teenagers. Luckily Anabella has never had a seizure and is almost a teenager, so we shall see what happens. Lucia, on the other hand, is prone to them when she gets poorly, and she can get poorly very quickly. Her first seizure had me extremely worried, and calling 999 for an ambulance is something I wouldn't wish on any parent. It was important to call, though, and thinking back on it now, I remember the Lee Evans sketch about it from one of his tours. Maybe you know it – if not – google it. Lee talks about how calm the operators are and how you as the caller are all panicking and anxious, even shouting down the phone or maybe even crying, while they are just talking calmly. It wouldn't work if they got all hysterical like you.

I remember when I called the ambulance service saying that my daughter was four and had just started shaking violently on the sofa while she was sleeping. We had brought her home early from school as she had a temperature of 39 degrees. The operator said, 'Is her airway blocked and is she breathing?' I had no idea – I didn't even think of checking. I then checked by putting my fingers to her nose and listening while seeing if her chest was rising and falling. I started saying that she had opened her eyes but didn't recognise me or even where she was. She wouldn't talk, she just made some noises which I could not understand. She tried to get up and collapsed on the sofa again; she honestly looked like the child from The Exorcist. At that point, I wasn't sure if I needed a doctor or a priest. I was just waiting for her head to start spinning.

I'm asking where the ambulance is, and the operator confirms that the first responder is on its way. 'I don't want a first responder,' I say, 'I need an ambulance.' Lucia keeps making noises and her eyes are rolling around in her head and the operator is so calm and talking slowly, the odd word here and there, like you would talk to a child – you know the voice. I remember thinking, Listen, you stupid patronising woman. My daughter is dying, and I need some damn help …

The reality is that she was never dying; she was perfectly fine. I know this now: a seizure is the body's way of resetting, like when Windows crashes on your PC and the screen gets frozen (the famous blue screen) and you can't do anything (think of Windows 95 – those of you who are old enough, and you will know what I mean). So Lucia's body hits the reset button and then she is fine. Extremely tired, yes, and we need to monitor the length of the seizure and the recovery time afterwards. Nowadays, having gone through this a few times, there is never any panic in our voices. Anabella and Sofia are aware of it and have witnessed it a few times also. They all have their roles. Anabella gets the medical bag, Sofia gets the phone in case we need to call 999. Either Alison or I record the time of the seizure and recovery. Someone moves dangerous objects out of the way. An adult places Lucia into the recovery position and places something soft under her head (if able to do so safely).

Back to the first responder. The medic arrived and checked her out. Her temperature was normal now, after she had been on the sofa asleep for three hours with a temperature of 39 degrees. One thing that's for sure is that a seizure is quicker than Calpol or Nurofen to bring a temperature down, but I wouldn't recommend it as an ideal option. The medic requested an ambulance, as it was her first seizure, and along with her genetic disorder, he wanted a doctor to check her over.

Riding in the ambulance, Lucia was out of it. Less than halfway there, though, with the lights flashing and the sirens going, she sits up from the bed and is sick all over me. The driver asks if it is serious enough to stop the ambulance, and the other paramedic says no, as Lucia was not convulsing and had already gone back to sleep on me. We carry on and the other paramedic and I clean her up as much as possible, and then we arrive at the hospital.

We go through the magic double doors that you see on Casualty (Holby City for the younger generation) and straight into the ward, with a bunch of wires attached to her. I get pushed to the side along with a chair, and just stand there, off to the side, waiting and watching all the activity around her.

She wakes up and says, 'Daddy, where am I?' 'In hospital, baby,' I say, and I sit on the bed with her. We just sit there and rest until the doctor shows up. She is not classed as an emergency anymore, which is good.

The doctor comes and explains that the seizure is a way of resetting her body and that now, after this one, she will be more prone to seizures. 'Keep an eye on her,' he said, 'she will be extremely tired for a couple of days,' (it ended up being nearly a week). 'Any seizure of between forty-five seconds to a minute, call 999; and if she gets too hot then try to cool her down quickly to reduce the risk of seizure.'

We added this to the long list of other issues with Lucia on her care plan at school, so they were aware, and this is now a normal part of Lucia and our caring of her. The good news about her seizures it that, for her, they are not unpredictable. For her, it happens when she gets over-excited (pressure on her defective heart) or when she has a high fever. The medical team agrees that she does not need medication to control her seizures.

What is a seizure and what is the cause?
Seizures are caused by abnormal electrical activity in the brain. Of course, we all know that – don't we! I had no idea, even after Lucia had one. I had to research exactly what happens in the brain. It can cause a temporary loss of consciousness (a 'blackout'), the body to convulse, unusual movements, and starring spells. Two factors identified to be common but not always contributing factors are lack of sleep or a high fever.

Seizures can be controlled by medication – anticonvulsants. If seizures are frequent and unpredictable, medication would be a very good option.

I will not discuss the pros and cons of medication. It is neither my place, nor am I qualified to make a medical argument. However, as a parent and someone who made the decision originally not to place Anabella on medication for her ADHD and then reversed that decision, I believe that it was the best thing for Anabella (although not me). I will say that you need to look at the person who may need medication and then make the decision or give advice based on their needs and not your own. It is very easy to make the decision based on your needs, and if you are a carer then you may well put yourself first.

The battle between myself and my wife at the time, regarding Anabella's ADHD and whether medication would be the answer, was a battle we had for a long time. We had lots of discussions with doctors and other family members who had taken medication for ADHD before we made our decision. We did consult Anabella as well (maybe not as much as I think we should have, with hindsight), and the decision made was based on her needs and her future development.

Trust yourself and do not be afraid to change your mind, but ensure that you give whatever decision you make a chance first. Not every doctor will be right, not every type of medication will be the best one, and your decision may not be right. It does not matter – it is a process. You have to go through the process to get the best solution for your situation. Everyone is different, and circumstances are often very different. There is no right or wrong here.

Communication difficulties:

Communication is challenging for a number of autistic people. Again, the issue varies in degree, from severe to minor.

Some of the key aspects in children are listed below, although this list can equally apply to adults. Some signs or symptoms are easier to identify than others.

- Limited speech or non-verbal
- Unable or finds it difficult to express their needs and wants
- Literal interpretation of words, direction or meaning
- Echolalia (repeating a word or phrase that has been previously heard)
- Loss of words which one was previously was able to say

• Inability to identify objects (poor vocabulary development)
• Difficulty answering questions
• Limited attention to people or objects within their environment
• Poor responses or lack of response to verbal instructions
• Disruptive behaviour – to gain access to, or avoid, items, activities, people and places.

The difficulty I have found over the years I have been reading, studying and researching how to help my daughter with her autism, from both my point of view and hers, is that some of this is entirely subjective. Difficulty answering questions, for example. How would I know if that is any different to any other child? Some children can answer questions, others need more information; some may understand the question but may not have the vocabulary to answer it. All children learn at different rates and that has nothing to do with autism or any other condition.

I have taken the view that I will try to help Anabella with anything that comes along as I would normally do, and not focus on or even add her autism into the mix. She will work that part out herself. I will keep trying to explain a question in as many different ways as I can, try new techniques and approaches until I find one that works for her. Sometimes Anabella seems to understand whatever scenario she is struggling with.

Luckily she has teachers at school who understand that she may need additional help processing information or having something explained in a different way.

Social Difficulties – Communication and Interaction:

Lets explore the social difficulties that autistic people have. This is one of the key things to understand in seeing how they perceive the world. And equally important, how the world perceives them.

Autistic people have various difficulties interpreting both verbal and non-verbal language. There is usually difficulty understanding gestures and tone; and many have a very literal understanding of language and will think what a person says is exactly what they mean. Imagine a world where politicians actually said what they meant! Maybe we should elect some autistic politicians.

Because of the very literal understanding of words and the difficulty interpreting non-verbal gestures, it is very hard to use and understand areas such as facial expressions, tone or pitch of voice, as well as jokes and sarcasm. This can give the impression that an autistic person is selfish and does not care about others.

Within the scale of autism, you also get many people who are non-verbal or have extremely limited speech. They will therefore use other methods, such as visual aids or sign language. They will often understand simple instructions and directions, yet may struggle with vagueness and abstract concepts. They will find it difficult to express what they what to say.

Others may have very good language skills in terms of speaking clearly but will still find it hard to understand the expectations of others within conversations. They might repeat what someone has said, or just not understand what others are saying, and so talk at length about their own interests.

When speaking to an autistic person, I would recommend that you speak to them in a very clear and concise way. Allow time for them to process what you have said. I try to speak in a simple way to Anabella, and I ask colleagues to repeat what they have said to me in a more simplistic way. You need to make things simple to understand while not treating someone like a child. The more open you are with someone, the sooner you will find that balance. There will be misunderstandings and extreme reactions at first, but through communication and being open, honest and not reacting, you will find a balance.

In terms of interaction once you understand the communication side of an autistic person, you can develop a special relationship. The difficulties you have read about above are around 'reading' a person, a situation or the gestures used in a conversation. Therefore, interaction can be limited.

It is hard for autistic people to navigate the world, at school and work, or in other groups. They struggle to understanding others' feelings and intentions, and to express their own emotions. As a result, they may appear insensitive; they tend not to seek comfort from others and will look for time alone when overloaded by people, or act and behave 'strangely', or in a way which is socially inappropriate.

Others may find it hard to form friendships. Anabella loves meeting people and being involved; however, she is not sure how to create friendships with people, as she is unable to read them and not sure how to act during a conversation.

I have moments where I am in the middle of a group and talking, and then I either lose interest in the conversation or become unsure of what to say, as no direct question has been asked. So I look around the room and feel awkward, and I then want to be alone. I just walk off. And that can be seen as socially inappropriate and insensitive to the rest of the group.

I can understand how it is deemed inappropriate; however, it is difficult to remain in a situation where you feel uncomfortable or anxious. The most difficult part is explaining why you feel uncomfortable all of a sudden. What has changed within the group? Sometimes nothing. Perhaps the conversation has just gone on for too long. If someone feels anxious, no one expects them to stay in a place or continue doing an activity that makes them feel that way. You would normally say that you feel uncomfortable and then leave or change the situation. An autistic person may not be able to do so. They may get so anxious that the only option that they can see is to walk off to calm down. They may show subtle signs, or even extreme signs, that they are anxious. Sometimes they respond well if they are asked if they are okay. A direct question which they can respond to can help the situation; and even if they then still leave the group, they may have felt able to say that they felt anxious, and are therefore more likely to return when calmer. Otherwise, they might feel that they could not return, and that others in the group were negative about them because they had walked off without a word.

Restricted and Repetitive Patterns – Behaviour, activities or interests:

How about the patterns which autistic people have that are 'restricted' or 'repetitive'? Some of these actions are the first thing a person may notice, and can trigger how they will be perceived.

Autistic people like routine, as the world can be a very unpredictable and confusing place. Daily routine sets up an expectation. You may travel to school or work the same way, leave the house at the same time, eat the same thing for breakfast every day. I do not think autistic people would make good covert spies. They are too predictable.

Rules can be important: things that you have been taught the 'right' way to do. The idea of change is not something that is easy for an autistic person to deal with, unless they have been prepared for the change in advance.

Anabella needs to be prepared quite a bit in advance when something big changes. Her transfer to secondary school was something we readied her for during her last summer term at primary. Over the course of six months we slowly introduced the changes that would happen. Things such as walking to school. The size of the school. The different subjects, the fact she would have multiple teachers. All this so she was aware of the changes way in advance, to give her time to process the information. If she had any questions, we all had plenty of time to answer them. She went to the secondary school to see the SEN teacher and had a one-to-one tour of the school.

We got her coloured folders so that each subject would be colour-coded to enable her to identify it quickly. It also enabled her to keep each subject organised. Once the timetable was provided on her first day, she decided which colours would be for which subject.

Many autistic people have intense and highly focused interests. These can change over time, or be lifelong. They can be anything from art or music to trains or computers. Some interests can be unusual. Imagine an autistic person who collected rubbish – not that unusual at all. Now imagine being a person who helps to encourage and develop that interest into recycling and environmental issues. Think of the amazing things an autistic person could think of around improving recycling and benefiting the environment, if their interest is channelled in a positive way.

It is good to encourage an autistic child or adult to channel their interest into something like studying, voluntarily work or paid work. It is often reported that the pursuit of their interests is fundamental to their wellbeing and happiness. Everyone wants to feel valued. An autistic person is no different in that regard.

I love maths and problem-solving. I got involved with computer coding when I was younger, building computers and writing programs. I have done this ever since. My first paid work was as a data analyst working with large complex datasets. Over the next ten years, the data has got bigger and bigger and more and more complex with project management. All this is fundamental to me, as I must feel that I am improving the process or contributing to the company I work for. I need to feel that I am making a difference.

Identify the interest that is key to you or to the autistic person you know. Try and encourage it as best as you can. Anabella loves acting and playing characters; this has been her main way of escaping and getting out of situations she did not like. She would create stories, her own imaginary world, and be drawn into it – drawn in so much that she truly believed that her world was real. She got extremely upset when that view of her world was challenged.

As a result, we have placed her in a drama school. Hence, her fundamental interest is encouraged and channelled in such a way that she is also taught the difference between fictional characters and real life. Along with support from her counsellor, we have managed to get Anabella to understand her imaginary world was exactly that. Imaginary. She can now introduce her imaginary scenarios into drama productions, and as a result she has become a better actress.

Disruptive behaviour:

I have lots of personal experience of this issue, including being disruptive myself in certain situations, and have had some very challenging behaviour from Anabella.

The main thing to try and understand is that this behaviour is normally an attempt to either avoid or gain access to a situation. And this is nothing more than what a child without autism would do. If a child wants a biscuit, they will ask and then play up a little when you say no, and you manage the situation and teach the child that that is not how to behave. The child learns over time that disruptive behaviour does not result in getting the biscuit, and may result in losing something, like a toy or timeout.

An autistic child is no different; the hard part is to remember that they do not always remember or learn, and therefore the behaviour repeats. It may vary, and in the case of Anabella, she does not react as much anymore and most of it can be easily managed; however, they are still times when she reacts in the extreme.

In December 2015, the family went to Disneyland Paris for a long weekend and stayed in the Disneyland Hotel. Absolutely amazing – and the family needed that break, after the last few years of hospital, operations, etc. – but the extreme reaction came, from seeing Jack Skeleton (a.k.a. Pumpkin Jack).

Jack Skeleton is the main character from The Nightmare Before Christmas. He is the Pumpkin King, in charge of Halloween. His job is to scare everyone in the world on Halloween. Spoiler alert – if you don't want to know, skip the rest of this paragraph! He gets bored and decides to steal Christmas by kidnapping Santa Clause. He dresses up as Santa, he calls himself Sandy Claws (he is the Pumpkin King after all) and attempts to deliver the presents instead. The problem is, the world he lives in is Halloween, so they take away the nice babies and replace them with monsters. As you can imagine, it doesn't end too well for the children. It is very good; I recommend you watch it – but maybe not with small children. You do not want them being scared of Christmas!

Anabella loves that film; we watch it every Christmas and she loves Jack the most. He is one of the characters that you can go and visit and have your picture taken with. We have special disability cards which allow us to get a timeslot without having to queue up. (Lucia's back is not strong enough to stand still for long, and Anabella can get very restless with nothing to distract her for long periods.) We got a timeslot before our lunch with the Princesses. The timeslots are normally given at ten-minute intervals, with only one disabled family per ten minutes to keep it fair to everyone. Now here comes the important bit in terms of the dialogue and how Anabella understood the situation.

So we queue up in the special line with our cards, and the lady gives us a timeslot of 3:30 p.m., and we have our lunch with the Princesses at 2 p.m. We check to see if this is enough time to do both. The lady is unsure, so recommends that we move to the 4 p.m. slot instead and allow another family to have the 3:30 p.m. slot. Anabella then repeats the instruction (her echolalia in action) that she has lunch with the Princesses at 2 p.m. and then comes back and sees Pumpkin Jack. The lady says yes.

Anabella then skips away happily and we go to lunch with the Princesses. Afterwards we started to walk back, took a wrong turning, and then found our way back to Pumpkin Jack. The queue was really small, maybe fifteen people in the line. We had just missed our 4 p.m. slot, and sadly we couldn't join the line, as the slot had ended at 16:15 and it was now 16:17. Anabella freaked out, screaming and crying like someone who has broken their arm or been cut open. The whole of Disneyland seemed to stop and stare as I got down on my knees and tried to calm Anabella down. Think of the scene from The Truman Show where everyone stops to change the frequency in the centre. It was exactly like that.

Hysterically crying and screaming, Anabella didn't understand why she couldn't see Jack, as he was there, and the lady had said she could. The fact that the slot was over did not register with her. She repeated the instructions given earlier. Lunch with the Princesses, and then see Jack. She kept screaming and pointing at Jack, shouting that he was there. There was lots of crying, and while looking around she spotted the lady who had said she could see Jack after lunch with the Princesses.

Anabella pushed me away, but I had a good grip on her shoulders, so I just wobbled. Anabella then decided to punch me in the face. I can say now that it was a good hit. Solid, direct, and one I would have been proud of myself if I had not been on the receiving end. I let go of her and fell to the floor. She ran off. I struggled up, thinking she was going to run away somewhere to hide and cry (as she does), but instead she ran directly to the lady and started screaming and crying at her, saying that she had said that she could see Jack and why can't she see him?

You can imagine the thoughts of everyone around: spoilt child, totally disrespectful child. Parents have no control. Their child would never behave like that. I think that if you had seen it, you might have thought the same thing. I know I did when I saw a child playing up like that before I had Anabella and when she was younger. Now I look at situations before passing judgement. The fact is, no one really knows the background to a situation. Maybe the child is autistic, and the parents are aware of it; maybe they are not aware, and have no idea why their child is acting up the way they are.

Alison spoke to the lady and explained what the issue and why Anabella was reacting the way she was. I had Anabella still in my arms, still crying hysterically. The lady came over to Anabella and explained that if she calmed down then she could see Jack.

Anabella then switched to being really excited, knowing that she would see Jack, but was still crying. It took me nearly ten minutes to calm her down enough for the lady to let her see Jack Skeleton. While sitting on the wall opposite Jack, waiting, she was slowly starting to settle down and be responsive. By responsive, I mean acknowledging others and listening to simple instructions. So the lady comes over and says it is her turn to see Jack. She jumps off the wall and runs straight at him.

Jack is a tall character, so the actor was on stilts; yet Anabella just runs straight at him and hits him square in the chest and hips and he gets knocked backwards. Luckily there was something behind him to stop him from falling over. He talked to her and about the film, and Anabella could answer all his questions and enjoyed her ten minutes with Jack Skeleton.

For the rest of the holiday, it was nothing but jumping and skipping around and shouting out at the top of her voice that she had seen Pumpkin Jack. It made her whole holiday so much more special, and even now she loves the pictures of her with Jack Skeleton.

As a parent, I have learnt that there are times when you must pretend you cannot see the disruptive behaviour, and other times when it appears from nowhere and simply hits you for six. It is never easy, and I wish I had the answers for others in this situation. The fact is, I don't – I'm still trying to find them out for myself. You just have to deal with whatever situation occurs at the time. Sometimes even the adults do not understand. The behaviour is more than likely a reaction to something, an extreme over-reaction in some cases, but still a reaction, nothing more. But if you yourself react, it will not help. That doesn't mean that being calm will help either, but getting frustrated or expecting them to understand certainly won't.

You have to fight the battles you can win, and in my experience this is not one of them. You just have to show them that you are there for them, that you are always a safe place, and whatever it is it should pass. Once it has, then you can look at it afterwards and see if there might be a way to stop the situation occurring again. Speak to the autistic person and find out if they understand what happened and if they think they know what might help them next time. They may not, but you cannot know until you ask them.

6 – A DAY IN THE LIFE OF AN AUTISTIC GIRL – WELL, MORNING ACTUALLY

During my working career I have been heavily involved in employee working groups helping people with disabilities. During one of my contractual roles, the working group had a platform which allowed employees to write blogs/articles and post them around the company.

I got heavily involved with one of the working groups and wrote numerous blogs during my year there. I wrote a series about being a parent caring for children with disabilities, and also about my own condition. I had never blogged before, so this was a new medium that allowed me to connect to people who may be interested. It was also the basis and framework for this book, as suggested by colleagues reading my work.

One of my articles was about a morning routine which, for whatever reason, didn't go how Anabella expected it to, and the resulting meltdown that followed. This was a normal weekday morning whereby I was getting ready for work and the girls were getting ready for school.

Her primary school experience was very bad. She was very badly bullied at school and was not helped by the school very much, as throughout her time there she was labelled one of the 'troublemakers' and 'attention-seekers'.

This was all before she was diagnosed with moderately severe ASD and ADHD. At one point while in year five (aged nine) she tried to take her own life at school. This was more of a cry for help, but nevertheless, not a very nice situation to have to deal with.

So, fast forward two years and Anabella has gone to a secondary school which only four others from her primary school are attending. Everyone else has gone to another school nearby. She is super-excited.

We go and meet the SEN teacher (SEN is Special Educational Needs), who has oversight over ALL the children in the school who have a complex or special need (regardless of how big or small). Anabella loves this teacher. He has a daughter who is nearly an adult with ADHD, so he understands the hyper side of this condition and how Anabella could get in class. He is also her teacher for history, which helps to give her structure and routine.

She has only been at school for a month but in that short time she has got herself a job in the library, and got a minor role in the school drama production for the winter term. She has made several friends (including older years and sixth form) and hasn't scared them away with her severe lack of understanding of personal space. When I say severe, I mean severe. If she asks an assistant in a shop for something, she is nearly standing on their feet, and when they move back, she takes two steps forward.

The biggest factor with autism is routine and structure. Without both, we are like little kids in Willy Wonka's Chocolate Factory, running around like headless chickens (which can be entertaining if you are watching from far enough away, but very scary if we are running towards you). When you are younger you get a lot of routine, but as you get older, routine is not as rigorous. We can normally adapt to the change, but for someone with autism, too much of a change or a sudden change can cause anxiety and the feeling of being unsafe.

Anabella's routine is to wake up at 6 a.m. to get ready for school. She must do the same things in the same order – if you try and change the order, or something is not ready when it comes to that activity, then potentially a meltdown could start. These meltdowns can vary in their extremity.

For example: she wakes up, then comes and sees me and finds out what I am doing after work. My after-work routine has not changed that much in the last four years, give or take the odd night, which she can manage. I tell her in advance if I know of a change. However, she still has to ask every morning; an expectation has been set.

She then gets dressed. She must put her clothes on in the same order. She then goes downstairs and has her medicine, followed by breakfast. Once she has done this, she checks her school bag. She has packed her bag the night before, but she must check it again to make sure she has everything. We try and promote as much independence as we can with the girls.

One day, her uniform was not in the place she would normally keep it. This was because she had a sports event after school the day before and came home in her PE kit. She placed her PE kit in her uniform place, and her uniform was still in her bag. After leaving me, she got frustrated that her uniform was not hanging up in the usual space. We found her uniform after five minutes, but the damage was already done for the morning.

Anabella was jumping around, not listening (more so than usual), and trying to get her sisters dressed for school (even though they wish to be independent too and can easily get themselves dressed). She tried to get them dressed as her own routine was disturbed and she felt that she must fill the gap with something similar.

She then had her medicine without any issues, and made her breakfast. Unfortunately, she made it wrong. She has Coco Pops and Frosties, but today she put the Frosties in first instead of the Coco Pops, so we had to start again (no one else likes Coco Pops and Frosties together, so the breakfast was not eaten). I have tried to explain that this was not a problem, and even told her to eat it. Never again. Seriously – that was like the beginning of World War III: the meltdown was worse than I have ever experienced before (except on the trip to Disneyland).

Once breakfast was made, Anabella got depressed and felt worthless because she got everything wrong. 'Everything' being: not hanging up her clothes the night before, making her breakfast wrong, and fighting with her sisters. She thought she was silly because she wouldn't eat the breakfast. It was very hard to get through to her that she was not worthless or silly and it was perfectly fine. We explained that we needed to find better ways of managing the meltdowns – but that's difficult when she is in that state of mind. It can take anywhere up to forty-five minutes to get her to calm down and get her self-esteem back.

At which point it is 7:15 or 7:20, and she is leaving late for school.

She leaves the house with me, currently. I can leave anytime between 6:30 and 7 a.m. The latest I can leave is 7:30 to get to work on time. We normally leave around 6:45 so Anabella can get to the school and have some alone time in the canteen and a second breakfast, before going to the library to help open it up for the students at 7:50.

We live approximately thirty minutes from the school, so we are normally fine to get to school on time. The problem on this morning was that she knew that I would normally leave the house no later than 7 a.m., and she felt bad that it was later than normal. She thought that she was making me late for work.

I am not as bad on the autistic scale as Anabella, although I choose to leave around 7 a.m. to miss most of the rush-hour traffic and commuters. I thus create a window to leave without getting too bad, but closer to 7:30 and I can start to get anxious, as I know it will be really busy and I could get to work late.

That morning, I spent the next twenty minutes while walking, talking and trying to calm her down before she left me at the junction where I go to the station and she turns off to go to school.

Depending on what else has happened during the day, her mood and behaviour can be even more extreme in the evenings. Her medication tends to wear off around 3 p.m. and the second dose only lasts a few hours. The idea is to keep her concentrating to allow for after-school clubs and homework. When her medication has all worn off, it sometimes seems like the whole world crashes down on her – most noticeably when she has had a bad morning.

I hope that this gives any parent or anyone who knows an autistic child some idea as to what can go on in their thought process. They are amazing children, and their thought process is unlike anything you can imagine.

I am very open around some of the amazing things that my children do. I believe that this is because they are different. I think it is good to share the main characteristics of their condition, even the worst things they go through, so you can appreciate the amazing things that they do. How something very small can make their day either the best – such as seeing Jack Skeleton at Disneyland – or the worst day ever, simply because of making breakfast wrong.

7 - ADHD

What about ADHD – what is Attention Deficit Hyperactivity Disorder?

Well, again, you could google it and find articles on the subject from all over the world. I must admit I needed more research into it, as before Anabella was diagnosed with both ASD and ADHD, her mum and I were unsure which one she had. I think Alison and I have lost count of the number of articles and information on both subjects that we have read. We tried to understand them in detail and decide which symptoms applied to Anabella. I believed she had ADHD/ADD, and Alison believed she had ASD. It turns out we were both wrong and right, depending on your point of view. (My daughter was greedy and wanted both of them!)

First off, there is a lot of debate on whether this disorder can be cured. There are various treatments available. Well, lets discuss that.

ADHD is a neurobehavioral disorder. Some studies state that it is as much as four times as common in boys than it is in girls, and can start as early as the age of three on average it is diagnosed when the child is seven years old, and there are three common subtypes.

These are: hyperactive, impulsive, inattentive, or a combination of all three.

Identifying the causes of ADHD is extremely hard and still there is no definitive answer. The causes have been linked to a wide range of different things from genetics, brain injuries, social or environmental factors, and even food additives.

As you can imagine, with such a wide range of potential causes, diagnosing the condition is even harder; but there are three core steps that are looked at:

1)   Showing that the behaviour is present in the child
2)   Showing that the behaviour at been present since at least six years old
3)   Showing that the behaviour in present in two or more life situations (school, work, home, relationship, etc.)

Treatment is an area which has been split between medication and non-medication. There are pros and cons with both, in my opinion. Even though Anabella is medicated for her ADHD it is not the only treatment that helps 'manage' her ADHD. For adults with ADHD, CBT (Cognitive Behavioural Therapy) is the preferred treatment, so if you have a child with ADHD like I do, do not think that medication on its own is the answer. It is not, it is a part of the overall treatment.

I think a lot of the concern in the medication debate has been over medication such as Ritalin, which has the side-effect of turning the child into a zombie. This is my opinion based on hearing from parents who used this with their child, and my own observations. Others who have given this medicine to their children feel that it stops the personality of the child coming out, hence the 'zombie' impressions. This is something that we did not want for our daughter, and therefore when we looked at medication we wanted to know the different drugs available and the side-effects of each.

After a while we selected a drug which we were told would not alter her personality (we love Anabella's personality, even though she is as mad as a box of frogs – which is a good thing). We were warned that it would be a long road with this medication. It would have to start with extremely small doses and then be reviewed and increased every three months. This was our choice, and we understood from the beginning that this would be a very long process. In terms of gauging her current level as well as the level that she needs to be, we are still in one of the three-month review stages, so nothing is fixed.

Anabella started on a 5mg dose, which produced no difference at all, as expected. This was then increased after three months and reviewed. When we got to 20mg doses, we started to see progress, which was also confirmed by the school. Her 20mg dose was split between a 15mg dose in the morning and a 5mg top-up after school to keep her focused enough to do homework and any after-school activities that she had.

This was done in the last few months of her primary school education and the summer holidays were generally good. Some evenings were very hard, with Anabella being very hyperactive, but generally manageable. Some days were not worth the battle and she was best left to be a little crazy, as long as she was safe and not hurting anyone. There would be events such as her being in the living room and jumping around like a three-year-old on chocolate and fizzy drinks – or imagine a five-year-old's party and how hyper twenty children are – that was Anabella all on her own. All that madness and fun (she can be extremely fun and playful in this mood sometimes) in one person.

Fast-forward to secondary school, and we have a meeting with the SEN to see how she is doing after the first month in general, and also about her medicine. The feedback is that during the last lesson of the day she is not always as focused as she should be. When it comes to after-school activities and clubs, we notice that the medicine does not seem to be lasting as long as it did – which makes sense if the morning one is not lasting as long either. Another factor may be that mental activities and processing may be more demanding in secondary school than in primary school.

Anabella's next review took place in November 2017 and it was agreed to increase both doses and change the type of medicine she took in the evening. We were also advised that the maximum dose per day would be 40mg. The doctors confirmed that they would not go over that; all parties were aware of this from the very first meeting over a year before, when medication was first discussed. From the outset, we were informed that this would be a long process and that Anabella would be given small doses which would then be increased to the highest amount allowed, and then reduced over her school life as she grew up and her body developed and she found new ways to manage her ADHD.

Her medication is now a 20mg capsule in the morning, which is a slow-release capsule. The after-school dose is now a 10mg tablet which is instant release. This means that she gets the hit of the medicine (like a shot of espresso, I suppose) which lasts for three to four hours (we hope) and then should be out of her system before she goes to sleep. Over a year later we, along with the school, agree that her medication does need to be slightly increased. We will have a discussion with the doctors over the best way to increase it. Will it be a 30mg morning dose and leave the evening as is? Or maybe change the evening one from 3 p.m. to 4 p.m.? Or increase both by 5mg? This is next stage of the process. In total, this has been an eighteen-month process so far.

Medicating Anabella was the best choice for her, I believe. It has allowed her to be more interactive with her peers (rather than be over-reactive), and more focused and able to listen to and follow simple instructions. It has allowed her to be more independent, and able to stay safe independently too. She walks to school by herself after she leaves me. She is aware of the dangers of the road. Alison and I were both nervous and reluctant to put her on medicine; I think we looked at it initially from our point of view and our experience of others. I will not insist that you should medicate your child, as I do not know your child, the situation, or how hyperactive they may be. I will say, though, that you should consider it while exploring all the options available.

I would class myself as extremely lucky in that the first type of medication we tried seemed to have a good effect on Anabella. I still see her amazing, if not slightly insane, personality shine through. The love she has, the fun and playfulness that has always been there, remains for me to enjoy in her company. Aside from being a lot calmer, she is still the mad crazy fun-loving girl she was before the medication. The major improvement, which was one of the main reasons that medication was decided upon, is her sense of (or lack of) danger. Remember her impulsive running away if you tried to hold her hand? Now, with the medication, she is not as reactive. She still doesn't like her hand being held for a long period, but she does not run off impulsively, and can manage it for a short while.

Remember that everything you, your child or your friend is going through is a process. It is a long, hard process, and I cannot stress enough that I would recommend trying each different approach, strategy or treatment, because you do not know what works or doesn't work until you try. Others may say it didn't work for them –

which is fine, but that does not mean that it will not work in your situation. Nor does it mean it will, but you will never know until you try. If you decide that a certain treatment is not an option, but other treatments are not working, I would encourage you to try it anyway. If nothing else has worked, what do you have to lose?

What are the symptoms of ADHD?
Just like ASD, the symptoms can vary. Some can be subtle, and others obvious. Each person is different, so they could present all or maybe only some of the common symptoms detailed below. These symptoms are normally common in children:

- Constantly losing personal items
- Daydreaming or 'tuning out' – inability to focus, easily distracted
- Difficulty completing tasks
- Difficultly processing information or following instructions
- Displaying emotions which could be seen as inappropriate*
- Impatience – unable to wait his/her turn in a game or wants to know the ending of a film
- Interrupts conversations
- Non-stop talking
- Verbal outbursts when frustrated
- Makes careless mistakes
- Constantly moving, touching things or disturbing others to get a reaction
- Unable to sit still for more than a few minutes
- No apparent regard for consequences of actions

*It is hard to judge 'inappropriate behaviour', as this is subjective and societies view change over time. What I personally believe is inappropriate is my interpretation, and depends on the circumstances and situation in which the behaviour is expressed. If I am with a group of eight to ten people at a work networking event, and for whatever reason I start getting anxious and need to get away and just walk off to stop getting worse and go somewhere alone to be with myself for a while – is this inappropriate?

Regarding adults with ADHD, it is harder to define the condition as most adults learn how to suppress symptoms and mask behaviour.

Symptoms could be very subtle and could easily be missed. Also, how the symptoms manifest themselves in an adult will be different to a child.

As ADHD is a development disorder, it is presumed that is cannot develop in an adult without it being present in childhood. The symptoms may be subtle in childhood and manifest into something more obvious in the adult.

An example of this would be the daydreaming of a child, leading to poor organisational skills and continually starting something and then never finishing it. Verbal outbursts could manifest into mood swings, being irritable and having a short temper. Finally, there could be a selfish attitude: the person might take risks, with little or no regard to their personal safety or the safety of others.

ADHD from childhood to adulthood – What are the stats?
The reality is that the research into adults with ADHD is limited and is often misdiagnosed – confused with other conditions such as depression or bipolar disorder, as with those two mental health conditions there will also be impulsivity, poor concentration and habitual symptoms.

The estimated stats seem to suggest that by the time an adult reaches twenty-five, 15% of those diagnosed at childhood still have a full range of symptoms. An estimated 65% still have some symptoms that affect their daily lives.

Is ADHD a learning disability?
A question I saw a lot while researching ADHD was whether the disorder is a learning disability. There are many psychological conditions which can affect a person's learning, but these are not always considered a learning disability. ADHD is one of those conditions that is not deemed a learning disability. It is, however, often confused with several forms of learning disabilities.

Around half of children and adults with ADHD have an actual learning disorder as well, such as dyslexia, and this makes it really hard to identify which condition is causing the learning disorder.

In summary, a learning disability is a permanent condition that develops in childhood, but can be largely overcome. Equally, ADHD is a condition that many must deal with and manage long into adulthood.

My opinion is that ADHD is a learning disability, especially in a child, since a child with ADHD is unable to learn to the best of their ability. Sadly, at the current time our schools are extremely stretched, and our government is failing. The younger generation and others who need additional help are not getting it, child or otherwise.

I think that it is important to understand a condition. It is vital that different approaches are identified and researched to find the best ones for the individual. There will be more than one approach, and not just medication, for your child, or yourself, or if you are supporting someone you know with ADHD. There is nothing wrong with trying new techniques or approaches to manage any one of the symptoms. It is a process; some things will work, others won't. Some may work for a time and then stop working for whatever reason. And maybe things that didn't work before will work now. Just give it a chance. You have nothing to lose.

8 - ADHD CHARACTERISTICS

There are three primary characteristics of ADHD. These are:

• Inattention
• Hyperactivity and
• Impulsivity

The hardest one to diagnose and the one must commonly overlooked is inattention, as this is less often disruptive to others. However, there are consequences. A child with inattentive ADHD will not be shouting around the classroom when they want a pencil or have been asked a question in class. They will, however, be spoken to around their performance in school. They will normally under-perform in relation to their peers, perhaps not following the directions set by the teacher. They commonly clash with other children at playtime, for not waiting their turn in games or not following the rules of a game.

Hyperactivity is one that is very difficult as well. Kids are hyperactive. Young children are always running around the place. They are exploring: new things, new textures, new smells. They have grown, and no longer crawl. They can speak. They feel like they are a big child now and not a baby. As a result, they want to do everything, and normally all at the same time. Boys tend to more hyperactive than girls; they always seem to have endless amounts of energy.

When a child gets to the end of their pre-school life and is about to start or has started in the reception year of a primary school, they have usually learnt to pay attention to others. They can sit quietly when instructed (for a limited period of time) and not blurt things out. They can wait their turn in games and answer when addressed. So at this stage we may not see a lot of hyperactive or inattentive behaviour.

The characteristic that stands out for teachers – and I would say for parents – as a sign of ADHD at this stage, then, is impulsivity. The blurting out, the dangerous climbing with no regard for their own safety or safety of others. The strong reactions to situations, which could be hitting out physically, or verbally insulting another child or even a teacher.

Looking back now, I should have recognised the signs when Anabella would refuse to hold hands and would run about in the road. I was so focused on keeping her safe and on her not following instructions that I did not think about it being impulsive.

It is hard thing to do; as a parent I am focusing on keeping my children safe and raising them to be independent young ladies, so they can manage whatever situation they find themselves in.

Inattention:

Being inattentive does not mean that the child is not paying attention at all. They can focus very well and their attention can be fully engaged on subjects they have an interest in. They may have no trouble staying on task and have good concentration levels. However, a topic that they do not have an interest in will cause them to zone out extremely quickly.

A possible reason why this is difficult to spot is this very good engagement and attention on one topic, and then no engagement at all on a different one. It could be seen as simply not paying attention, as opposed to an underlying ADHD symptom.

Another common symptom is the bouncing around from task to task, without actually completing any of them; or skipping necessary steps in those tasks. Children with ADHD find it very difficult to organise their schoolwork and their time compared to their peers. ADHD also makes it very difficult for them to concentrate on something when there are other things going on around them. They tend to need calm, quiet environments in order to stay focused on the tasks at hand. They can get very easily distracted by noise or movement in a classroom. Someone else talking across the room could distract them.

The five common symptoms of inattention in children are:

• Having trouble staying focused; easily distracted, or bored with a task before it's completed
• Appears not to listen when spoken to
• Difficulty remembering things and following instructions; does not pay attention to all the details or makes careless mistakes
• Has difficulty staying organised, planning ahead of time and finishing projects; and finally:
• Frequently loses or misplaces items, such as homework, books, toys.

Hyperactivity:

This is the most obvious outward sign of ADHD. While children are naturally active, they do have quiet periods. Hyperactive children do not seem to stop moving. They will bounce from one task to another and try to do several activities at once, even when they are in situations that could focus them, like sitting on the sofa or on the classroom floor. This will be very difficult, and they will feel the need to tap their feet, shake their leg, fingers constantly drumming.

The five common symptoms of hyperactivity in children are:

• Constantly fidgets and squirms
• Has difficulty sitting still, playing quietly, or relaxing
• Moves around constantly, often runs or climbs inappropriately
• Talks excessively
• May have a quick temper, a 'short fuse'

Impulsivity:

Impulsivity can cause problems with self-control. Children with ADHD will censor themselves a lot less than other children do. They will interrupt conversations, invade other people's space, ask irrelevant and/or inappropriate questions in class. They will make tactless observations and blurt things out, maybe ask overly personal questions of strangers and adults. Instructions such as 'sit still' or 'be quiet a moment' are twice as difficult to deal with as they are for any other child.

Children with impulsive signs tend to be very emotional. They can be moody, and tend to overreact as well. As a result, the child is generally viewed as disrespectful or a troublemaker. A weird and needy child.

The five common symptoms of hyperactivity in children are:

- Acts without thinking
- Guesses, rather than taking time to solve problems. Blurts out answers to questions in class without being asked or waiting for the whole question to be asked
  - Intrudes on other people's conversations or games
  - Often interrupts others; says the wrong thing at the wrong time.
- Inability to keep powerful emotions in balance; results in angry outbursts, temper tantrums or crying fits.

We have explored the three main characteristics of ADHD. I would like to discuss four positive traits that a person with ADHD could have. If these traits are focused and directed in a positive way during childhood, then the possibilities are endless.

Creativity:

Children with ADHD can have amazing creative imaginations. They may be daydreaming, but inside their head they will have ten different thoughts at once. They become a problem-solver, trying to resolve each one of those thoughts. They will have lots of different ideas to resolve one problem. They get easily distracted, but the positive side of this is that the distraction that they notice is normally not seen by someone else.

That creativity could be used to be an artist. To write children's stories, like Roald Dahl. Think of the inventions of Willy Wonka during the tour of the chocolate factory. The snooze-berries are fantastic! I'm not sure where or how the idea of a mobile phone came about but someone must have thought of it. Everyone said in the early 1990s that it would not last, it was silly. The phones were too big – who would use them? Nearly thirty years later, nearly everyone has one. Consider email and such things.

Flexibility:

Children with ADHD can consider lots of different things at once. They have multiple ideas and can flip back and forth between those ideas. As a result, they can be open-minded and not fixed on a set path to solve a problem. They can come up with alternatives and identify things that others have not thought of.

Enthusiasm and spontaneity:

A child with ADHD is never boring. Constantly moving, they are interested in everything and anything new that they can see and do, until such time that they work it out so that it is no longer a puzzle anymore, or fall in love with it because they understand it. They have so much enthusiasm to bring to the world, and this can be infectious. They can bring life to an event that may be extremely challenging and make it fun.

Energy and drive:

Along with their enthusiasm for things, they bring tons of energy. They also bring drive and determination. Towards things that they have an interest in, they are extremely hard-working and want to succeed. They will focus on the task until it is completed. They may get so focused on a task, that it may be difficult to get them off that task and onto another, especially if the task is an interactive or hands-on.

Finally, I would like to talk about why a child with ADHD seems to be impacted in school more than in any other situation. Let's have a look at all the characteristics of ADHD and the school learning environment. First off, ADHD does get into the way of learning. It stops the information being taught being absorbed. It is difficult to learn if you are running around the classroom or not paying attention to a task because it does not interest you at your core.

The school environment is set up for learning. That is its core function. It does this by setting up an environment where children are required to sit still, listen quietly, not distract others. Children need to pay attention and follow instructions; concentrate on the tasks given to them.

This all makes sense. The problem is that all these things are the very things that a child with ADHD struggles with. Not because they are unwilling, as they can focus on specific interests. It is because their brain will not let them.

This does not mean that a child cannot learn and develop at

school. It just means that teachers, parents and the children themselves (depending on their age) need to evaluate their strengths and weaknesses and come up with creative strategies and techniques which will help them to stay on track, keep them focused on the task at hand. If this happens, the child will learn to their full capability.

Anabella is hit-and-miss during some of her school lessons. At the start of some lessons, she is very distracted and talks excessively, and then it takes a while to get her to settle down. At which point, she is not fully focused for the rest of the lesson and her learning suffers as a result. Nowadays she has a task first thing, when she goes into class. She is tasked with getting all the reading material out and handing it out to each student. If there are print-outs, she has to hand these out as well. She also sets up some of the teacher's things on her desk.

This gives Anabella focus from the start of lesson. It also gives her more of a vested interest. She has given all the books out. She was responsible for setting the teacher's equipment up ready to teach. Anabella therefore feels that she has to perform well for the teacher. She has been given responsibility and does not want to let her down.

Sometimes the smallest thing can have a huge impact.

9 - A DAY IN THE LIFE OF AN ADHD CHILD

It is hard to describe a typical day of a child with ADHD or autism or any other condition. There is no typical day. Every day brings a new situation and reaction.

The one constant with Anabella and her ADHD is the relentless need to get involved. It could be a conversation between her mother and me, her sisters. The dog is calmly lying down – she feels she has to be involved. One of the girls asks for a drink and she has to grab all the glasses or the drink from the fridge. If she has not got something to do, or even if she has something to do, she will position herself in the middle of things.

This can be extremely frustrating for all parties. People think that she is bored and that if I give her something then she will calm down. I have tried that, and it doesn't work.

I read a story about a mother with a young daughter with ADHD. She was about three years old and sitting in the trolley while queuing up waiting to pay for a few items. She keeps grabbing all things from the trolley. Eventually grabs some crisps. The mum takes the crisps away and the child's tantrum starts.

Of course we understand that a young child will generally react when something is taken from them. It is part of the learning that a child has to go through. However, this child was uncontrollable. She screamed, shouted. She stood up in the seat, trying to climb out. She hit the mum when she was trying to keep her safe. Her mum refused to give in, and the longer she held out, the louder and more dangerous the child became. The mum had exited hundreds of shops due to her daughter's behaviour, and food shopping brought the worst outbursts and meltdowns. The shop was very quiet, everyone staring. The other customers were shaking their heads. Even the staff were raising their eyebrows. There were still two other customers in the queue ahead. Always when something like this happens, everything seems to take longer. The mum explained that it felt like everyone was looking at her for ten minutes, when in reality it was probably only a minute or two. After the hundredth time trying to calm her down and putting the child back in the seat, a lady behind them shouted, 'Oh for the love of God, give the damn child a biscuit to shut her up.'

Sadly, this reaction is more common than I had realised. The lady's shouting is something that we have experienced a few times when Anabella is having a bad day or a meltdown. The looks and shakes of the head, however, this is far more common. I understand how it looks from the outside; I will admit that I, sadly, have done my share of head-shaking, before I had children and even after the girls were born. It is very easy to judge. It seems, in the world of social media and reality TV shows which are designed to judge people against each other, that it is acceptable to compare your life to someone else. That person has more money than me. This family has it all. This child got better grades and has more friends than mine do. Comparing yourself to someone else is not healthy in my opinion. It does not change your situation. Now, ambition – seeing what someone else has, like their role in a company, and you feel you want to be where they are in three years – that is not unhealthy. It is good to have a goal. The person in the position you want to be in is the best person to talk to, to find out how they got there and what you need to work on to do the same.

Back to the mum in the queue, now almost crying after being accosted by the lady and her child screaming. She said that she could have handled the situation better. She could have been nicer in her response. She could have explained that her daughter has severe ADHD and therefore it was very difficult. She could have explained that she was a single mum of three children and worked part time, and was doing the best she could.

She could have done. Instead, the reaction was to turn around with tears streaming down her face and shout back: 'She is three years old and you need to mind your own f***ing business.' She then grabbed the trolley and rushed across to the self-serve checkout. She just stood there by the trolley, crying with the child still screaming and shouting for the crisps which had been taken away from her.

Sometimes, it does feel like that: everything can be so overwhelming that it feels too much, and I can relate to the feelings of frustration felt by the mother. I have got to that level of frustration before; I remember a time when someone said that my child was not very well behaved, and I should be ashamed of myself. I was in shock when I got told that. I was a young parent and Anabella was little. It was when we first started to believe that something was affecting Anabella. I was being spoken to by an older woman with her children, and it was very difficult for me to process what was happening. I just stood there, very much like the mother thinking she could explain the issue and then exploding. I did not do anything. I just stood there unable to speak. Maybe this is part of growing up. I was in my early twenties. Now, over ten years later, I would handle the situation very differently.

From every situation that you find yourself in, you can learn, and react differently if you find yourself in a similar situation again.

Anabella has described her day as adventure and chaos being constant friends. Most days she describes as a rollercoaster, with highs and lows. Extreme highs and manic lows. How these feelings make her feel like a genius at times, and at other times extremely stupid. Extremely distracted while working on tasks that cannot hold her interest, and hyper-focused on tasks that can.

Her morning routine is to wake up at 6 a.m. with her mobile phone alarm. She jumps out of bed and then gets ready. However, if for whatever reason the alarm does not go off, she gets up late. Even if it is just five minutes late, restlessness kicks in. She is more easily distracted. She forgets about her medicine and has to be managed to ensure that she takes it. She then needs help to calm down until the medicine kicks in.

School is great for her, as schools work to a schedule. Schools starts at the same time and her lessons start and finish at the same time every day. This allows her to focus and realise that nothing will be late. The weekends, however, are not all the same.

During school terms, she and her sisters go to drama school. This is held at her secondary school and is a familiar routine every

Saturday morning. The afternoons are always different and depend on what other activities the girls have on, or the chores that need to be done. This is when the reactions take place – over-reactions mainly, either to a TV show, a film, or even playing with the dog.

Her second lot of medicine is due to be taken around 3 p.m. Around thirty minutes before is when her medicine starts to wear off. At this moment, she is unaware that her medicine is wearing off. She does not recognise her behaviour and reactions changing. She gets frustrated more easily. Finds it difficult to form words. Talks excessively, about anything that comes into her mind, or creates a story based on whatever word she overhears or reads.

She gets over-excited and tired, and then when she gets into bed she says the same thing as she does every day. She will do better tomorrow.

10 – HOSPITAL POEM

Here is a poem Anabella wrote as part of her English lesson at primary school. It was selected and published in the Young Writers' Once Upon a Dream book.

This poem relates to one of Lucia's many operations in her early years. Most of her operations have been successful, although recovery has not always been successful.

The poem made Anabella's mum cry out when she first read it. She rang me at work in tears and had me thinking something serious was wrong. After I read it, I was taken back by the amazing power of the piece, and it gave me more insight into how Anabella felt while Lucia was lying in the hospital.

Hospital
As I drift off to sleep
My mind starts a jigsaw
Piecing together a dream about my sister.
She is in hospital, lying motionless in bed.
Not a sound to be heard from her amazing little head
I am with my family and friends who are cuddling me tight
But without her here and chatty
I feel empty inside
She might be there for weeks, maybe months, maybe years
Or she might not come home at all
A few weeks later, as I sit there on the bed
I hear a cough, a chuckle, a laugh
As I see her awake, I feel happy and relieve as we dance together.
As I wake up, we snuggle up together
Safe and sound.

Anabella Russell (10)

11 - DIGEORGE (22Q11 DELETION) SYNDROME

Lucia has a genetic condition called 22q11 deletion syndrome, also commonly known as DiGeorge syndrome.

What is 22q11 deletion syndrome?
This is an extremely complex syndrome and there is still lots of research to be done in terms of the impacts and symptoms it presents. This is a life-long condition, similar to autism. There is currently no cure or treatment for the overall condition.

Symptoms vary greatly from individual to individual, as does the severity of the condition. The simplistic version as to what this syndrome is as follows. A piece of genetic material is missing from the child during the stages of pregnancy. This is not a result of anything the mother has done or not done during pregnancy. In about 90% of cases, the missing part of the DNA was either from the egg or the sperm. It is not usually passed down to a child from their parents, but it is in a few cases.

Where there is no family history of the condition, the risk of it happening again to other children is very small. In the case of Sofia, who was born two years later than Lucia, we had multiple scans and checks during pregnancy to see if she might have it as well. All those checks were negative.

The stats for DiGeorge are that if neither parent has the condition then there is a less than 1% chance that your child will get it. Lucia was in that 1%. However, if one parent has the condition, the risk of passing it on is 50% with each pregnancy. Meaning that if Lucia decides to have children, there is an even chance that each child she has could get the condition.

Some children with this condition can be extremely ill and very occasionally may even die from it. Many others grow up without even realising that they have the condition at all. Usually it is diagnosed after birth, by a blood test checking for genetic faults; however, this is not a common condition so it is not generally part of the genetic testing. The test is only done if there has been this condition in your family in the past, as there is a higher chance of having it. There are some physical traits that may be seen as indicators; a blood test would be used for confirmation.

What are the symptoms of this condition?
This is a question which is very hard to answer without further research being done. Great Ormond Street Hospital has a special DiGeorge Clinic, where Lucia has been for check-ups and some of her tests have been reviewed. The team at GOSH have provided advice based on results of their previous experience of other children with this condition. They are also continuing to conduct research.

Most people with DiGeorge will not have all the issues associated with it, as it varies greatly from individual to individual. Here are five of the most common issues, and some other, less common issues that an individual could have:

- Learning and behavioural problems
- Speech and hearing problems
- Mouth and feeding problems
- Heart problems
- Hormone problems
Other possible symptoms:
- Higher risk of contracting infections
- Bone, muscle and joint problems
- Short stature
- Mental health problems

What treatment and support is available?
As previously discussed, there is no treatment for DiGeorge. However, individuals are closely monitored to check for symptoms, as not all are present from birth. Some symptoms can even develop during adulthood. The overall condition of DiGeorge is not treatable, but some of the symptoms can be. For example, palate issues can be corrected with surgery. Lucia has had four different operations to correct her palate and is now going through multiple rounds of speech therapy to re-teach her palate how to pronounce sounds and

work her muscles correctly.

Regular hearing tests, blood tests, heart scans and lots of measurements of height and weight are some of the things which identify other issues. In this way, hearing loss and immune defects can be identified. Palate issues were identified as one of the key issues why Lucia did not put on weight as a baby. Her growth, or lack of, was the indicator. Lucia has regular check-ups for numerous things, just to check that they are not getting worse and that nothing new has developed. As this is a genetic disorder and she is still developing, anything is possible. As the check-ups have shown a steady position for Lucia and everything seems to have levelled out, she is now reviewed only on an annual basis until she hits puberty.

As Lucia was diagnosed very early, we applied for an educational statement during her time at pre-school. This statement is reviewed every two years while she is in mainstream school. We also got dietary support straight after being diagnosed, due to her lack of growth and her inability to take in milk and solid food. We were provided with special high-calorie milk, which she still has now to maintain her weight and give her energy to keep going throughout the day, especially when wearing her back-support brace.

Physiotherapy was key for Lucia to build her core strength up. She still has physiotherapy, which is now extended to improve her fine-motor skills, finger movements and keep her core muscles as strong as possible while wearing her brace.

Lucia also has infantile scoliosis, and the support she has received since this was identified has been amazing. The specialists who look after her conduct regular x-rays to see how her spine is growing. They want to ensure that the spinal curve is not getting any worse. Sadly, the battle before this was identified took over a year, a year in which we kept saying to her physio team that she was still bent over while walking; not standing straight, and still leaning to the side. After all the therapy, this area was not improving. What I found equally frustrating was that things took so long. Health professionals do not seem to want to admit that they do not know something or that they could be wrong. Could this be to do with all the compensation claims and liability issues? Who knows. What I do know is that the problem was spotted by a doctor after we demanded that someone else take a look. He took Lucia's top off and spun her around and said immediately that her spine was severely curved. No physio took her top off, to my knowledge. If they had, maybe they would have spotted it.

The team were so focused on trying new therapy techniques or saying we needed to give it more time, at no point did someone suggest going to a back specialist or even discuss it. The bottom line is, I am a parent, I am not a medical professional, and I am solely reliant on them knowing what to do. In my work, if I am unsure, I find out who might know and ask them; no one treats me like I am a failure for not knowing. I do not get into any trouble at work; I form an opinion based on the facts and the experience and skills I have. If it is a legal issue, then I ask a lawyer or the legal team. I do not assume that my opinion about the law is correct when I am not an expert. It seems that many people don't want to admit that they don't know what is going on and thus appear less than they are. They would rather do nothing than try and get someone's help. Of course, you tend to only see the worst via social media, so I would not read too much into that. But it is out there, and as a society we should try and break that trend.

The main reason we should try and break it is the fact that it does not help. History is full of examples of things changing and developing, and it is a good thing. If unsure, the majority of people can accept that you may not know, and are therefore happy to see someone else for their opinion. What people cannot accept is evidence that someone is still not improving, or feeling that their concerns are not being taken seriously. No one wants to make a mistake and admit that they do not know; but sometimes that is the best thing that could happen so that a new approach can be looked at.

It seems that society is pressuring everyone to get everything right first time. This is not practical or helpful. Focusing on one thing on the basis that it worked for someone else is not the answer. Things develop through trying new ideas, new approaches, and being open-minded.

What is the outcome for someone with DiGeorge?
Everyone is different, and it is difficult to predict how severe the condition will be. Also, symptoms could develop late and may be aggressive.

Usually, as you get older, symptoms such as heart and speech issues tend to become less of an issue; however, behavioural, learning and mental health problems could continue or even increase.

The risk with any disorder that has a behavioural impact is that when you get older, the behaviour is then seen as a personality trait, such as being defensive or aggressive, which is not always the case. Of course, people can be passionate about a subject, and during a discussion could be defensive over a point of view. This is a reaction to a specific point in most cases. For people with a behavioural disorder or a behaviour symptom within a disorder, this is normal daily behaviour. They do not see it as defensive or aggressive. It is therefore difficult for them to explain why they behave like that. It is the same as asking them why the sky is blue. It just is.

One of the key things that is very difficult to resolve with anyone that has a behavioural issue is the ability to communicate. The person with the behavioural issue may not see it as an issue. Therefore, they may be unable to communicate the reasons for their demeanour. The other person may then not be able to communicate either, as they may feel hurt or upset by the comment. Emotions, especially when heightened, make it hard to think, or be clear through actions, gestures or words. It is hard enough without a behaviour disorder, so think of how hard it must be for someone who may not be able to communicate well physically, someone with a palate issue, say. That is why we see a high rate of broken or failed friendships and other conflicts in the lives of people in such situations.

For Lucia, it was very difficult before her palate operations and during the early ones, when her speech was still very difficult to understand. She was quiet and got very frustrated with people who did not understand her. Because of this, her drama teacher was allowed to accompany her when she took her drama exams. The reason for this is was that the examiner would ask her questions about her piece of work and would be looking for certain words and a clear understanding of what she was doing and what her character was meant to portray.

This was extremely difficult at first, as the drama teacher did not always understand what Lucia had said. I was not allowed into the exam. Lucia got a little frustrated with the examiner and her teacher at certain points during the first two sets of exams. Because of her condition and the fact that she was young, she was given extra time and the examiner was lenient.

Often this kind of leniency seems to disappear when you become an adult. As an adult, you are supposed to have developed, and therefore understand. This is true in some ways, but we are always still learning. Just because I am an adult, why should I know how to interact with another adult who has Parkinson's, for example? I do not. I do know a lot about the condition, aside from some knowing some famous people who have had it. But I do not know, in any great detail, how the disease works. How it affects someone. How best to interact with a person who has it. Why should an adult be able to have complete control of their emotions in all situations? If you look at social media, you will see a lot of videos of road rage and people losing control, or commenting that someone should have known better. But you only know when you have been taught or have learnt. You cannot know what you do not know.

12 – DIGEORGE CHARACTERISTICS

Lets explore the characteristics of 22q11 deletion symptom in more detail. We will look at some examples of what difficulties someone with DiGeorge could have, and how Lucia has dealt with some of her symptoms. At one stage Lucia had nearly twenty different specialists looking at different aspects of her care.

Learning and behavioural:

Learning difficulties could bring issues such as delays in walking or talking. It could also be a longer-term learning disability, such as ADHD or ASD.

Lucia had several difficulties when learning how to walk. She consistently fell over when changing surfaces. This included stepping from the grass onto the path in the park. She would even fall over just walking along. Of course, when standing and taking their first steps, a child will fall over a lot (well, mine did). Some children who do not have any conditions are slow learners and can be very clumsy. Not all children work to the same timeframe. But they learn.

Some behavioural problems can be the result of a different underlying issue; in the case of Lucia, she used to get extremely frustrated and then shout and hit out when she was younger. The underlying cause was her inability to speak clearly, and her behaviour was a reaction to getting frustrated. When she tried to explain what she wanted, no one could understand her.

When looking at any issue, be mindful that it could be a symptom of a different underlying issue. It might not be, but it is worth investigating, as you could be spending a lot of time trying to reduce or remove a behaviour trait without addressing the true cause.

Speech and hearing:

These issues can be temporary or permanent. Someone with DiGeorge will have a temporary which could be caused by frequent ear infections, or have permanent hearing loss. They could also be slow at starting to talk and may have a 'nasal-sounding' voice.

Lucia was diagnosed with a left-ear problem. Not full hearing loss, but partial hearing loss, sufficient to warrant her wearing a hearing aid. She also had 'nasal-sounding' speech, which resulted in many palate operations and speech therapy, which is still ongoing.

Her speech issues, along with her inability to communicate with any clear sounds or words, resulted in some very disruptive behaviour at pre-school and during her reception years at primary school.

Lucia would be able to hear the majority of words spoken to her. She would also be able to understand the instructions for the morning and what she could and couldn't do at pre-school, including having to ask to do certain activities. She would try to explain what she wanted to do, but the teachers were unable to understand her. This would result in her grabbing the item she was asking for, or hitting out.

She would also get very upset if she had followed instructions but was then punished for her behaviour. An example would be when she was at primary school. They were taught that if you wanted to get scissors or any craft material, then to ask for it. She asked a teacher if she could do some crafting and have scissors. The teacher was not sure what she had said. Lucia then grabbed the scissors and got into trouble for grabbing the equipment. This was very confusing for Lucia, as it would be for anyone. You follow instructions, and rather than a reward, there is a negative consequence through no fault of your own.

Mouth and feeding:

Individuals with DiGeorge could have a cleft lip or palate, which is a gap in the top of the mouth or lip. They could have difficulty feeding and might bring food back up through the nose.

Lucia was born normally, meaning that she was not induced early or late. She was born naturally, not c-section. There were no known issues identified during pregnancy or post-birth. However, within the first two months she would hardly eat anything and spent a lot of time sleeping. Despite numerous discussions with health visitors and explaining that we believed something was wrong, they did not believe there was an issue. They concluded that as Lucia was on the lowest point of the weight-height graph but within the 'acceptable' range, she was fine and there was nothing to worry about.

Just because you may be in the 'acceptable' range for growth does not mean that everything is okay. All children develop differently. It does not mean that there isn't something else wrong. The biggest challenges come when you feel that something is wrong, and you have no evidence. It was very difficult to know where next to go after not being successful with the first health professional. And it seems that I am not alone, given my discussions with other parents, colleagues and friends who struggled to be taken seriously about a feeling they had. One test comes out negative, or you fall within an 'acceptable' range, and your concern is classed as invalid. This is very similar to when Anabella was classed as a troublemaker because of her behaviour, before diagnosis. And still some teachers and assistants did not believe the diagnosis. I do understand that we cannot always keep testing until you prove something, but not to test or explore other possibilities is wrong. A parent's concern is not invalid. It should be investigated. Sometimes you may need to be forceful with health professionals, to make them refer you and take your concerns seriously. We believed that something was wrong, but were equally aware that neither of us were doctors. It is important to always be open-minded and listen to feedback, and then go to the next stage. In the case of Lucia's feeding, we chose to see a doctor after the dismissive behaviour of the health visitors.

Heart:

Individuals could be born with heart defects from birth (congenital heart disease).

After numerous back-and-forths with health visitors who, in my opinion, ignored us and did not take our request seriously, we ended up going to see the doctor at the hospital Lucia was born in. The initial issue was her feeding, or lack of. Still no progress, even after changing her milk and speaking to the health visitors.

We took Lucia at three and a half months old and explained the issue of her feeding, and the doctor checked her over. He found a heart murmur and admitted her to hospital that day. So the lack of feeding turned out to be a serious heart issue. The hole in her heart was the reason why she slept a lot, due to excessive pressure being put on her heart, and this pressure was high during feeding. Another reason while she was not feeding for long was that the pressure on her heart was too much and so she went to sleep.

The doctor also noticed some other extremely subtle things in her face, such as a long oval shape and 'fingers'. It was enough for him to suspect DiGeorge and request a blood test to confirm. The test came back the next day along with an x-ray of her heart and confirmed the DiGeorge syndrome. The x-ray also showed the 3mm hole in her heart. 3mm does not seem that big when you look at it on a ruler, but that size is large for a new-born baby who had to wear clothing for premature babies.

Lucia ended up having open heart surgery at four and a half months old. This was done at one of the best heart hospitals in England, the Royal Brompton Hospital in Fulham. Lucia had a VSD (Ventricular Septal Defect) repair in September 2008 and the operation was extremely successful. The doctor repaired everything over the course of four to five hours and then she was back in intensive care for recovery.

The whole process, from seeing the doctor and being diagnosed to her heart operation, was four weeks. That gives an indication of how seriously the doctors and surgeons viewed her heart issue.

However, Lucia's recovery was not very successful at all. We were told that she would probably stay in her drug-induced coma for a couple of days to recover after surgery. After that she should start waking up on her own, or they would look to slowly wake her up with drugs and monitor her progress.

Three days later and there was no change at all. The drugs were reduced in an effort to slowly wake her body up. Sadly, instead of waking her up, it did the opposite. It stopped her body. Her body crashed and her heart flatlined and therefore needed to be restarted. She was brought back and left alone for the rest of the day. This happened twice more. The fourth time they tried, Lucia reacted in the way they wanted. She started to slowly wake up, and a few hours later she was moving slightly and trying to cry out.

Due to the complications that took place in recovery, the doctors and surgeons has some serious concerns. They warned us that although the operation had been successful, they were nervous about how her body reacted during recovery. As a result, they were not sure if her body would be able handle the pressures of life in general. The heart was still very weak. Although the repair had relieved the pressure on her heart, they still advised us that she might not survive past December. The surgery took place at the end of September.

Hormones:

Individuals can suffer from shaking tremors and/or seizures. This is a result of an underactive parathyroid gland (hypoparathyroidism), which is common.

Lucia does not have an underactive gland; however, she has had a few seizures. The main reason why she has had seizures is her getting high temperatures. A seizure is a way of resetting the body clock. Lucia's body would be struggling to regulate her temperature, so the seizure kicks in.

Risk of infections:

Some individuals can be prone to picking up infections. This is a result of a compromised immune system. The infections could affect any part of the body. They could be ear, chest, or even throat infections.

All children, especially when they start going to nursery and primary school, get infections. Part of growing up and being exposed to other children is the rite of passage of colds and infections. Lucia is no different to any other child. She is no more prone to infections, and yet, when she does get an infection, she is extremely up and down. She needs regular temperature checks, as this can increase very suddenly and if it gets too high then a seizure could happen. There is a special medical bag that we have at the ready for when she gets poorly.

Bone, muscle and joints:

With this condition, you could have multiple issues involving your bones, muscles or joints. It could present as pain that keeps coming back, such as leg or arm pain. Individuals could also have an unusually curved spine (scoliosis) and rheumatoid arthritis.

Lucia has got very aggressive infantile scoliosis. Her condition got progressively worse over a very short period of time. As a result, she now wears a removable brace which covers her torso. This is designed to stop the scoliosis getting worse; it is not designed to treat it. Luckily, she was very small when they first spotted her scoliosis. Over the years that she has been wearing her brace, she has been growing, and we are waiting to see if the spine will straighten out by itself when she hits puberty. She was first diagnosed with scoliosis back in 2014, and because of its aggressive nature they placed her in an upper body cast.

An upper body cast is difficult to explain. One way I can describe it is if you think of the plaster cast you get when someone breaks their arm. This is what she had to wear over her torso. This cast was shaped like a men's sleeveless gym vest. Think of a young Arnold Schwarzenegger is his famous yellow Gold's Gym top.

The cast restricted her from lifting her arms above her shoulders. Also, she was unable to take it off, so she had to sleep in it. To help her sleep, we got her one of those long pregnancy pillows. This enabled her to lie in as comfortable position as possible to sleep. She was unable to have a bath or shower, unable to go out in the rain.

She missed out on some school activities because of the cast as well. She was unable to do certain PE lessons, mainly ones that involved running or possible body contact with others. This was not for her safety, as she was not going to get hurt, but mainly for others. Due to how heavy and solid the cast is and how little she was, she ended up getting very tired. And because she was tired, her concentration was reduced. This meant that she could fall over or fail to stop while running, and hit another child, or vice versa.

She was also unable to do some of the other things that she loved doing. Things like riding her bike. The plaster cast was too heavy for her to balance well on a bike. It restricted her movements considerably and she was unable to pick things up off the ground. She was unable to climb, and some of the games that we played at home had to stop. The trampoline was stopped for a little while. The house is always loud and crazy with games, including play-fighting, which had to stop as well.

Lucia was always and still is smiling and happy, although there are a few moments in which she is very tearful and sad that she is unable to do things. Her sisters always help her with things as much as possible. The biggest problem is that Lucia is furiously independent. So much so that she will always try something first regardless of any discomfort or potentially how dangerous it could be for her. We do not want to rein in this independence at all, just try and channel it into the right way. So we change some things around the house to make it safer for her but preserve her independence. We put all the school things and school shoes in boxes, one box each for each child. We moved the things in the boxes around so that Lucia's belongings were at arm height for her, so she did not have to do any bending down or stretching up to get them, which she couldn't do. We also got a special chair for her as part of her therapy with the cast. We have two of these chairs, one for home and one for the school. The chairs were especially helpful when she was in her plaster cast; they ensure that she keeps the correct posture so that her spine does not get any worse. They also help her concentration and focus, as she is sitting correctly and is not uncomfortable.

Now she has her removable brace, there are some key differences. She can take it off, so she can have a shower and go swimming. We do not remove her brace very much at all, however. The more it is off, the worse her back will get. It is a cast that goes around her torso, so it does not restrict her movements. She can raise her arms above her shoulders. She can climb, she can also bend. It is still slightly restrictive, but nowhere near as much as the plaster cast. She is able to participate in all her school activities again, including PE. The brace is higher on her body than the cast, near her hips, but still doesn't allow full movement, to ensure that her spine is kept straight.

Lucia still wears her cast in bed. She must wear it for at least twenty-three hours a day. She has learnt to ride her bike in the brace, and we have even removed the stabilizers. She has fallen off while wearing the brace, but she gets up and carries on. She does get sore underneath the brace, especially during the summer months. Her skin gets very red, sore and clammy. When it is too much for her, we remove the brace for the day, allowing air to get to her body, and apply moisturiser. The next day, her brace is back on without any issues.

Short stature:

Stature is not just limited to height, although the majority of cases is fixed on just this. It is about the stature of the person as a whole. That could be difficult to identify if the child has short parents for example. Lucia's mother Alison is only five foot one, and I am not exactly a tall man at just over five foot nine. Lucia was never going to be a giant anyway. She is slightly smaller than her peers.

Lucia has a small body in general. She has small arms and not much muscle tone. She has not had very good core muscle strength, but over the last few years her core strength has improved dramatically with therapy. When the cast was put on, her muscles were not worked as much as they would be normally, due to restrictions in her movement. Her physiotherapy was increased to build that back up once the cast was removed. Her fine-motor function is still limited, too. Her therapy forms part of her daily routine, both at home and in school; it has been continuous since she was first diagnosed, and I cannot stress its importance enough. It does several things. Of course, the main thing is improving those muscles, but it does a whole lot more. Lucia now feels more confident that she can interact with her peers. She feels that she can do the obstacle course on the school's sports day: a child in a brace, running, bending and climbing with the others. Therapy is not just physical, and I could not imagine what position Lucia would be in without it: the special chairs, the different aspects of speech that we have been taught; how to improve her fine-motor skills so she can use a pen and pencil and write legible words.

Mental health:

This is one of the most underappreciated issues in society, and not only for people with Lucia's condition. There has, though, been a massive push for mental health awareness in society over the last few years. Personally, I think it is the most important thing of all. Not everyone has the tools or techniques to help them manage difficult situations mentally. Out of the twenty-or-so specialists that Lucia has, she does not have a mental health professional. Mental health in adults and children is so important for the long term.

In children the research is limited, and the statistics tend to show that adults are more likely to have mental health problems, such as schizophrenia or anxiety disorders. I would challenge this, though, and say that it is not more likely in adults. I know a lot of children that are anxious and have periods of depression, but I think that due to the limited research into mental health issues and children, it is potentially difficult to identify. Lucia, though, has shown an amazing mental attitude to her condition and the multiple operations that she has undergone. I would like to know why her attitude is positive.

Could it be based on the fact that since she was three months old she has been in and out of hospital? At one point she was in one hospital or another for a check-up or some sort of test nearly every week. And every year she has had an operation of some kind, many of them major. I do know that she has had some bad days. After operations she is sore, in pain and very tearful. However, children are very resilient and have short memories (especially when they ask for a biscuit and you say no; they come back ten minutes later, having forgotten you said no in the first place!).

Would a twelve-year-old girl who is now more curious and conscious of her body be able to stay positive wearing a full body cast that makes her look like a female version of Arnold Schwarzenegger? Would she be as comfortable as she was before, when she was going out with her friends, wearing that little red top in the summer sunshine with her scar running all the way down her chest, visible to everyone? Or wearing her brace, which is visible through tops?

Would a twelve-year-old boy who loves playing sports be able to sit and watch from the sidelines, unable to play any sports (especially contact sports) in his cast? Seeing everyone else play and knowing that he was good enough to play but was unable to?

I would say that the majority of kids and young adults would be able to. They would have some down days, of course they would. Who would not, going through everything that they go through. I still believe as life goes on that many people find a way to deal with whatever situation comes up. If one shop does not have any bread left, then you go to next one, or you go without that day.

My concern is that mental health often seems to come last on the priority list. When a child has a down day, she or he needs help, and sadly it is either not available or not adequate. The young adult who is struggling to come to terms with a temporary or permanent change maybe needs more help than others.

I have seen a lot of focus around mental health over the last few years, both at the companies in which I have worked and in the media. In 2016 and 2017 all sorts of different people seemed to be talking about mental health – celebrities, senior members of parliament, companies, all explaining how important it is.

A lot of people have asked me how we manage in the family with all our different conditions. How do we manage the multiple hospital appointments? people wonder. I once said that we manage because we have no choice. This is not strictly true. There is always a choice. At every turn you can either do something or not do something. And there is always a consequence to each choice you make. The choice is that you deal with it or you don't. I say I have no choice because the alternative, not dealing with something and running away, is NEVER a choice to me.

Lucia's issues:

Lucia is a young child who has dealt with so much in her ten years. I am sure that there will be more challenges to come, both in terms of her condition and life in general. She has a lot of symptoms, but she is still smiling, trying, and mainly succeeding.

She does not let her condition get her down. She does not let anything (or anyone, for that matter) stop her trying something new. She wanted to ride a bike without stabilisers after being told that it would be extremely difficult due to her brace/cast, her inner ear issue and her core balance issues, and she proved them wrong, just as she has always done. She proves everyone wrong. Doctors, teachers, and especially her parents.

I have been told several times by people listening to my talks or reading my articles that they could not imagine being in my shoes and doing what I do. I find this a hard thing to process, if truth be told, as it is all normal for me. This is my life, there is no alternative. I do not do anything special, in my eyes. I am just a man who is a father to three amazing little girls, two of whom need help to manage two very complex conditions.

You should try stepping in Lucia's shoes for a day and a night. Maybe the night after her open-heart surgery, with the doctors trying to wake you from the coma, your body rejecting the idea of waking up and having your heart restarted. Or how about an afternoon when she refused to come into the house until she managed to ride her bike. Hours of trying to ride her bike with her brace, getting grazed knees and hands because she kept falling off, and then, when she finally got to ride her bike, going round and round laughing and screaming with joy all evening. Finally, imagine her on a regular school day after she has been to the hospital to have speech therapy in the morning. She gets to school and has to catch up on the lesson she missed; she then has lunch. Then, running around the playground with her friends, another child accidently runs into her. Back into class after lunch, then start the physiotherapy. After physiotherapy, which lasts around fifteen to twenty minutes, she returns to class activities. After a long day wearing her heavy brace, her body is so tired. She is mentally and physically drained. She continues to sit in her special chair and refuses to give up on that final task set by the teacher.

13 – A DAY IN THE LIFE OF A GIRL WITH DIGEORGE SYNDROME

A typical day starts at 6 a.m. Stretching out on the bed, Lucia has to slowly turn over. If she is wearing her plaster cast, she has to negotiate her way around her large pregnancy pillow to get herself into a position to climb down the ladder from her bed, as she is unable to bend. In her removeable brace it is a lot easier, but she is still unable to bend fully.

The first thing is a check of her skin under the brace. The brace is removed, and any heat rash is checked to see how bad it is. If it is really serious and sensitive, then her brace is left off for the day. Her body is moisturised completely, especially around her hips where there are bruises from the brace. One side of her chest seems to get more heat rash than other areas, and is creamed fully. The brace is curved around her hips, but it is constantly rubbing against her hip bones. Therefore she is covered in bruises and her skin can be raw.

The brace is put back on after ten minutes and she gets herself ready for school. She puts on her own school clothes and then comes down for the morning physiotherapy session. This therapy covers two things. One is her fine-motor movement. The therapist called it 'finger gym'. She must move her fingers around in specific ways. She holds a pencil and uses other tools to develop her flexibility. She spends ten minutes doing this. After that, she starts doing her stretching for her back and to develop her core muscles. This is all done while wearing her brace. We use a giant gym ball. She lies on her back and rolls it back and forth. She slowly tries to go as far back as she physically can. She also sits on the sofa with a smaller ball and picks it up off the floor and then twists her core and places the ball to one side. This continues for a few minutes. All the while she is developing her core muscles and back to keep her balanced and give her the strength to wear her brace.

At this point it is around 7 a.m.; it is time for breakfast and then off to the hospital for her weekly speech therapy, which starts at 8. On the half-hour drive Lucia reads her books. She reads out loud, to work her throat muscles ready for therapy. Arriving at the hospital, we go straight into the therapy waiting room. Just before 8 a.m. her speech therapist arrives from the other side of the hospital. Lucia jumps off her chair and runs to her and gives her a cuddle. She has been her therapist for nearly six years.

Inside the therapist's room, Lucia picks the games that she wants to play while doing her speech therapy. Her favourite is a game in which you have to pick matching socks from a washing machine, very much like Snap. The therapy is that before you have your go, you have to say a word or two words that contains the letter or letters which are being practiced. At the moment Lucia is focusing on the 's' sound. She must add a 't' sound in front of it to train her palate muscles to get into the correct positions for different sounds. Therefore, the words are not the same as how we would say them. Lucia is really good at this. I, however, am not so good, as I can say the 's' sound correctly, so it is harder for me to say it with a 't' at the beginning. It is important that we know how the sound should be said so we can correct her when she is at home.

At school, she has an assistant to help her. Her assistant also comes to the hospital maybe once per term or when the letter changes, so that all parties know how Lucia should be talking and we can correct her.

After therapy, which lasts an hour, she goes straight to school. Lucia is generally very tired after the morning as she has had to concentrate hard, and she sometimes has a little sleep in the car or reads her book out loud again while practising her sounds.

She arrives at school between 9:30 and 9:45, so only misses the first lesson, which is maths. She is given the work to do as homework, so she does not miss anything. Lucia gets sad about missing her maths lessons. It is her favourite subject. There is a morning break of twenty minutes which starts at 10:30. Her lunch is 12:15 until 13:00. After lunch, she has her second session of speech therapy and physio. Straight after lunch, she is taken out by her assistant and they practise her speech for about fifteen-twenty minutes and then do fifteen-twenty minutes of physio as well. This is done every day. Normally the teacher explains the lesson plan straight after lunch so Lucia understands what she needs to do when she returns after her therapy session.

The rest of her afternoon at school is no different to everyone else. She has her lessons, does her work, and if she has PE then she does PE with everyone else. She keeps her brace on. After school she comes home, and she starts working on any work that she has missed or not finished due to her therapy sessions.

She also has after-school events, just like any other child, and at the end of the day she is completely shattered. Her body is very sore, too, and she can get quite emotional.

The most uncomfortable periods are around lunchtime play during the summer. The heat makes everyone hot and sweaty, and the sweat gets trapped under Lucia's brace. The lack of air reaching her body is the main cause of the heat rash she gets, which is why when her body is showing signs that she needs a rest, the brace is not on for the whole day and night. The other issue during the summer is that her skin is very itchy. She knows she is unable to take the brace off and she admits that she gets frustrated over this. Her back also becomes sore and she looks forward to having a quick shower as she knows that she can take her brace off for another fifteen minutes. As well as the moisturiser, she also has special eczema cream for her itchy skin. Lucia enjoys her time without her brace in the shower or being creamed.

Over the course of a really hot day, she can have her brace off for a maximum of forty-five minutes. Lucia is very disciplined with her brace and will only ask for it to come off if she is in a lot of pain. She has worn the plaster cast just once and she knows that if she does not wear the brace she could end up in that again. She does not like that idea at all as it really does restrict her movements and her social interactions. She generally can't play games, as the risk of serious injury to another child is high.

Lucia has special equipment to use at home and school to help her learn. She has special pens and pencils. The pencils are a lot shorter than a typical HB pencil, as these are too long and heavy for her to hold straight. This gives you an idea of how weak her muscles are. The pen is the same length as her special pencils. It has a special grip as well which allows her to hold it in the correct position. Her handwriting has dramatically improved since we found these online.

When a child is tired and hungry they can get very emotional. Lucia is no different. At the end of a long day, she can become very needy, too; she loves her cuddles and we have a special type of cuddle when she does not have her brace on. It is called a 'squeezy cuddle'. This is when I pick her straight up in my arms and give her tummy a squeeze and she can feel it. She always makes sure that she gets as many of these as possible when she has the change.

Her confidence is growing; she now knows that even with her brace on she can still do, and mostly succeed in, what she wants to do. She does not allow her brace to be a reason not to try something. She does her drama shows in it, and has recently become the house captain for her school, now that she has moved up to year six.

There is no typical day for Lucia. Every day is different. There is always a hospital check-up or appointment due. Sometimes she has a seizure, or we get a call from the school to say that she is very hot and wants her brace off. There is always something happening. The main thing is Lucia is always smiling. She does not let anything stop her, least of all her condition and the various associated difficulties that she has to battle through every day.

14 – HOSPITAL OPERATION 1: OPEN HEART SURGERY

Lucia was born in April 2008. By June, we knew something was not right with her. She was not drinking enough milk and sleeping a lot more than Anabella did. We know all children are different and grow differently, but no child should be sleeping for nearly twenty-three hours a day and only able to drink half an ounce of milk, taking nearly twenty minutes to do so.

The health visitors were not worried. Yes, her weight has dropped from the graph line when she was born, but she was still on the bottom of the graph and so within acceptable range. We were told to try and change the milk, but there was no change in Lucia at all. In July we spoke to the health visitors again and they were even less interested with us.

Alison decided that she needed to take Lucia to a doctor to have her checked out. I was in Jersey, in the Channel Islands, for work, so I was not even close by. Alison took Anabella to her friend's house and said that she would be a couple of hours. Her friend asked her to make sure she was back before she had to do her school pick-up. Alison said that it should not take long. How wrong she was.

Alison had already seen the GP a couple of days before regarding the fact that Lucia was not eating and sleeping too much for a new-born baby and had said that we needed a professional to have a look at her. The GP agreed upon seeing her, and referred her to the paediatrician at the hospital where she was born. Alison arrived at the hospital on the Thursday. The paediatrician took a look at Lucia and then had a listen to her heart and checked her birth records for any complications. Lucia was born within about twenty minutes after arriving at the hospital, and there was nothing to indicate any issues during the birth.

After listening to her heart, he decided to admit her there and then as well as do some further tests that afternoon and into the evening. The first thing was a blood test. At this stage, we were not told what tests were being performed and Alison did not ask. She was still in shock that Lucia had been admitted with a problem with her heart. What the doctor had heard was a murmur. To confirm this, and also the extent of the heart issue, he ordered an ECG of her heart that day.

Once these tests were conducted, Lucia was placed in the ward and an NG tube was put down her nose and into her stomach. (NG stands for nasogastric.) The process is that a thin plastic tube is passed down through your nostril, then pushed down the oesophagus and into your stomach. This is then used to feed food or medicine to the patient. The tube was put in place so that Lucia could get high calorie milk inside her to help her gain weight while she was in hospital.

After nearly five hours in the hospital, Alison called Kim. Kim was fine about the delay, and said she had given Anabella dinner, and to come and pick her up when Alison was ready. Alison said she would pick her up in an hour, after calling everyone to let them know what was going on. She called me at just gone 5 p.m., when I had just left my colleagues to sort out my hotel and then go out for dinner. I got into my hotel room and my phone rang. I did not even put my bag down before I answered my phone. Alison was very shaken, I could tell by her voice. I managed to get her to calm down and then explain to me what had happened. She told me that Lucia has been admitted to Mayday Hospital in Croydon with a heart defect. She continued to tell me about the tests and the tube inside her to feed her, and said she should find out more information tomorrow. She told me that her sister Sarah and her boyfriend at the time would be looking after Anabella that night at our house. She was going back to the hospital to stay with Lucia, just packing some things. Sarah called her other sister, Katie, who was living out in Essex at the time, and explained what had happened. Katie and her boyfriend, Andy, drove from Essex that night and also stayed at our house overnight. Anabella had two aunts and uncles to fuss over her all night and day while Alison was at the hospital and I was travelling back from Jersey. I said I would get on the first flight home. I called work and explained what had happened. They arranged for me to get the first flight out of Jersey back to the UK at around 6 a.m. There were no late-night flights from Jersey. That was fine, Alison said, there was nothing I could do that night, and she had her sister arranging everything. No need for me to rush and cause more panic. I said I would go straight to the hospital from the airport.

I went out for dinner with my colleagues and told them what had happened to Lucia, and they made sure that I had a good evening and that no work was discussed that night.

I have a number of colleagues in Jersey from my years working in the share plan reward industry, so the majority of my night was spent wandering around the island and seeing old friends. I finally turned up at my hotel at around 1 a.m. and sat in the bar just thinking about Lucia. What would I do now? How would I look after my family? What did this mean? Would she be okay? The fact is, I had no idea, and there was nothing I could do to either find the answers or make Lucia better. I have learnt over the years that my time and energy is better spent focusing on tasks that I can control or influence.

Alison packed a bag for Lucia – nappies and a few clothes – as she was not sure how long she would be there. Then she settled down and waited for Sarah and Dom to arrive. Once they arrived, she said goodbye to Anabella and went back to the hospital to spend the night on the ward. Katie and Andy arrived later that evening. I understand that all four of them had Anabella up late that night playing.

I went to sleep around 2 a.m. having packed all my stuff; the hotel had ordered me a cab for 5 a.m. to drive me to the airport. I arrived back in the UK around 9-ish and made my way from Gatwick to Croydon, arriving at Mayday Hospital around 10:30 in the morning. I walked into the ward and saw Alison sitting in a chair just looking at Lucia lying on her back with a tube down her nose. She was wired up to a couple of machines, a stat monitor and something else.

The ECG had been done the day before, and the results showed that there was a clear issue with her heart. They were also concerned about her weight. We decide to go and get some lunch as Lucia was asleep, and talk about what we needed to do. Alison was still on maternity leave, so she did not have to worry about work, and I was not expected into work. I cannot praise my company enough, and especially my team and management, during this time. They were so supportive, and I cannot stress enough how grateful I am. Even though I have left the company, I am still in touch with my old colleagues and the management team who were so supportive of me and my family during this time.

At lunch with Alison, she explained that she had not packed a bag for herself, in the panic of getting everything for Lucia. She had to call Katie and get her to come to the hospital in the morning to bring her clothes and underwear. Now, thinking back over everything we as a family have gone through, we love to laugh about these silly things.

I decide to go home in the early afternoon as I had not slept a lot the previous night. I got back to our home in West Norwood and walked into the living room to find everyone sitting on the sofa and Anabella playing on the floor with her toys. All four adults looked worn out. They had that look of someone who has said they will look after your child for you and not realised how much energy they have, and are now looking forward to handing them back as quickly as possible. Alison and I were the first of Alison siblings to have children. It showed.

I said thank you for everything and gave them all hugs and kisses. All the while Anabella just stayed on the floor and didn't register anything. They said that they would take Anabella out if I wanted to sleep, but I said I was good. I wanted to play with Anabella. I had always played with her when I got home from work, and then put her to bed for the night. Being in Jersey the previous night meant that that night was one of the few times I had not put her to bed since she was born, so I wanted to put her down for her afternoon nap. I could catch up on my sleep then. Catch sleep when you can, I thought, as I was not sure when I was going to get a full night's sleep again.

Anabella and I played for a while and had cuddles. We had some food and then I put her to bed and then I went straight to bed too. I think I fell into a deep sleep before my head even hit the pillow.

Lucia ended up staying in Croydon for a week, mainly to get her weight up to an acceptable level. At the end of the week, her weight was just under average for her height and age. This was good. Then the fun started.

What I mean by this is that the doctors thought that actually she has been doing so well that maybe her heart was not as bad as we, her parents, thought. They implied that we were not feeding her correctly. They decided to take the tube out completely and weigh her at night time. This was done, and then she was left overnight. During the night, Lucia did not drink from her bottle – even the nurses on duty at night tried.

In the end five nurses try to feed her, including the senior nurse, who was the main person saying that we were not feeding her properly. Lucia did not cry very much during the night as she had fallen asleep after fifteen minutes maximum of the nurses trying to feed her. Eight hours, and she had only taken about half a fluid ounce of milk, which clearly is not enough. Now they agreed that there was not a problem with us: her weight had dropped, and the NG tube was reattached.

Alison and I were both trained how to put in the NG tube and tape it down. The nurses taught us how to use an NG tube to feed her. We had to check that the NG tube was in the right place and had not moved since the last time. We had to draw a little liquid from her stomach and then check the PH level using a litmus paper before feeding her. We would then feed her, slowly, a set amount, then wash the tube with sterilised water to clean it completely.

After the training, the doctor informed us that Lucia has been referred to the Royal Brompton Hospital in Fulham. This is one of the leading heart hospitals in the country. He had still not informed us of the blood test results, or what he had been testing for. Now that Lucia was a good weight and they were comfortable that Alison and I knew how to feed her correctly, they discharged us to go to the Royal Brompton Hospital. We were like outpatients.

We arrived at the hospital and saw Doctor Rigby. He was a heart surgeon and he arranged for Lucia to have another ECG and had a good look over her. The ECG was done very quickly and within an hour we were in his office and he was explaining what the scans showed. We could see her heart and we could see a space by her heart which he was pointing out. We understood the hole, but not its seriousness. He described it in a way that we have always remembered. He explained that Lucia's heart was the size of a 50 pence piece. The hole in her heart was the size of a 5 pence piece. In his office, he told us that it was serious and that an operation was needed, and quickly. She was not growing, she was not awake often enough, and she was not eating by herself. It was extremely dangerous and the stress on her heart would only increase. He advised that there was a high risk that she could die without the surgery. He told us that he would confirm the date for the operation that day, and that we would return in a few days to Mayday Hospital.

We returned to Mayday and the doctors were happy with Lucia in terms of her weight gain, and happy that both of us knew how to check the positioning of the NG tube, feed her safely and clean the tube. They wanted to keep us in for monitoring.

A couple of days later, we were informed by Mayday of the operation date at Brompton. The operation was set for just over two weeks' time. Mayday agreed that they would discharge Lucia into our care and we could take her home until the operation. This was the best news we had had in just over a week. We got support at home a few days later, a nurse checking that everything was okay. The nurse was happy, and ordered a few additional tubes, tape, syringes and milk. We would need to take the milk with us to Brompton to feed Lucia. We were told that if there were any issues with her tube at any time of the night – for example, if Lucia had pulled it out – we should just turn up at the ward and someone would help us.

It was so nice having that support from the hospital, and then packing up the bag in the ward and knowing that after a week we would finally bring our little girl home. It was amazing coming home and having our family all together again. Our extended family as well. Alison's mum, Patsy, was there (her dad was still in Gibraltar), and both her sisters and their boyfriends. Alison's mum ordered a large Chinese takeaway for everyone. The food arrived, the starters were set up and the first duck pancakes were made, all the family laughing and smiling and little Lucia sitting asleep in the living room and Anabella at the table looking for her food.

Then the phone rang.

Patsy answered the phone. It was Alison's granddad, Sam, on the end of the line. He had called to say that Pat, Alison's nan, had collapsed. The ambulance has just arrived, and they were on the way to hospital. He felt that everyone should go to the hospital. So pretty much during the starter of our takeaway, everyone got up and left, although Alison was told to say at home as we had just brought Lucia home a few hours earlier. The moment they all left, Alison was all worried and unable to sit still, so I told her to go too. It was her nan, and the girls were fine. Thirty seconds later Alison left the house and drove to the hospital to be with everyone else. Thirty minutes later, everyone including Sam was at the hospital and put in the family room. I have never been in this room at a hospital. Alison said it was a small room with a sofa, a few chairs and a little table. On the table were leaflets about residual homes and bereavement services. Everyone was there for twenty minutes before the nurse came into the room. She proceeded to tell the family that unfortunately Pat had passed away. She had passed away in the ambulance. They could go and see her now if they wanted.

Everyone came home close to midnight and no one was very talkative. I was still up, just sitting on the sofa. I had put the girls to bed and Lucia had been fed through the NG tube. We have always said that Pat was waiting for Lucia to come home before she went. According to Patsy, she was very worried about Lucia, and was praying for us to bring her home. She got her wish. Lucia was home.

We had two weeks until Lucia's operation, and had things to prepare for that. We also had Pat's funeral. Alison's mum was due to go back to Gibraltar once Lucia came out of the hospital, but she stayed with us to set up the funeral and then she was going back, as she had a cruise booked leaving from the United States just after the funeral. Alison said that she was not going to go to the funeral as it was just a few days after Lucia's operation.

I was extremely busy at work with a new project. In terms of Lucia, this was also very stressful. She was awake more now that she had more energy and a good weight. She did not stay awake as long as she should, but it was longer than before, so we got to interact with her more. Anabella also wanted to interact with her when she was awake. Sadly, when Lucia was asleep and so little, Anabella thought she could dress her up like one of her dolls. In fact, Anabella's doll was bigger than Lucia. As Lucia was awake more, she also cried more due to the tube; I believe she could feel it and was unsure what it was. She could also grab the tube, which she did a few times, and before we knew it the tube was out and then we had to go back to the hospital to get a nurse to put it back in. We did try putting it in ourselves; we had been shown how to, and we knew how to check the right position, but we were unable to do it. Lucia would cry lots and struggle, and Alison felt that she was hurting her. I was okay with the crying and struggling, I could ignore it and try to put it in, but I just never felt that the tube was going in and down correctly. Many a time during those two weeks I had to drive to the Mayday hospital in Croydon in the early hours of the morning to get a nurse to put the tube back in. Then it was home for a bit, a few hours' sleep, and then up early and back into work at 6 a.m.

When we took Lucia out back then, we got numerous looks from other children and adults. It was hard when I saw parents pull their children away when they asked about Lucia. It felt like Lucia was infectious; like if their child came into contact with her then they would get her condition. Back then I was very sad and a bit angry that people thought my daughter was infectious, like a leper, and should be hidden away and not allowed outside. I was young and felt that adults should know better. Now, ten years on, I would like to think I am wiser, more experienced and a lot calmer and more accepting of most things.

Children are curious, and the children saw something different about Lucia and wanted to understand. That is amazing. We did have a few parents and their children ask about the tubes and things. And that was fine, we explained as best we could and said that the tube helped her eat, as she could not drink a lot of milk.

One day, Alison and her mum were out in Croydon town centre. They walked into an M&S café with Anabella slowly walking next to them and Lucia sitting in a pushchair. They sat down at one of the tables, and Anabella climbed and sat in a chair. She had her colouring book with her and Patsy got drinks and a cookie for her. It was time for Lucia to be fed. The one good thing about having an NG tube to feed her was that it did not matter if she was awake or not. Alison started to prepare the milk and the equipment; Patsy had Lucia on her lap playing, as she was awake for a little bit. Alison got out the litmus paper and laid everything out on the table. On the opposite table there was another woman with her child. The child was around four years old.

It is unusual to see babies with tubes attached to them and having to use syringes, so it is not surprising that the little girl was curious. She was smiling at Anabella and Lucia, although Anabella was too focused on her colouring to notice. Lucia was looking around, sitting on her nan's lap while everything was laid out ready. Alison attached the syringe and started to draw liquid from the NG tube to check that the tube was positioned correctly in her stomach before feeding her. The syringe was very small and held no more than 20ml of liquid. It was important that the tube was in the correct place. The liquid drawn was then extracted onto litmus paper. The litmus paper showed what the PH level of the liquid was – how acid the stomach was. If the PH was correct then the tube was correctly positioned and Lucia could be fed.

The syringe was later changed to a larger version. This syringe held up to 250ml of liquid. The plunger of the syringe was not used: you allowed gravity to take the milk. The reason was that the NG tube was very narrow and therefore did not allow a large amount of liquid down the tube, reducing the risk of too much liquid too quickly going into Lucia. Someone using the plunger could push too quickly. Parents are not trained like nurses, and it is very easy to push too quickly. I am not sure exactly why. Maybe it is the emotion – parents are emotional. Lucia is my second daughter and was very poorly, so we needed to make sure that she took enough milk. It would have been easy to force it, thinking it was for the best.

Alison got Lucia's milk from the table and opened the bottle. She took off the silver sterile foil and poured half the bottle into the tube. Then she raised the big syringe full of milk high in the air, to ensure that there were no kinks in the tube. The young girl was looking on. She slid off her chair and started to walk towards Alison and Lucia. Patsy was holding Lucia while Alison was holding the syringe full of milk as high and as straight as possible and watching the milk slowly go down the tube.

When the milk in the syringe got down to the final third you needed to add more milk. You should not let it completely empty and then fill it again. So, near to that point, Alison gets ready to pour the remaining milk into the syringe. Meanwhile, the other mum notices that her daughter has left the table and is walking towards Lucia. She jumps out of her chair and grabs her daughter's arm and pulls her away. She pulls hard and fast, shouting at her, 'Come away, you shouldn't go near people like that.'

I am not sure what she meant by 'people like that'. Lucia is not contagious or infectious or any other negative word that ends in ious. Alison was taken aback, and after checking that all the milk had gone down the tube, responded by saying that Lucia was not infectious and was nothing to worry about, but would she like the woman to clarify what she meant by 'people like that'.

The woman was startled, I am guessing that she was not used to being spoken to so bluntly, and did the typical face when turning your nose up at someone, thinking that you are better than someone else. She packed up her things, and before walking away, she said what did Alison expect, being a hussy of a single mum with a drug-dealing father who was probably in jail. She then walked off, pulling her child along with her.

It is shocking that this sort of thing ever took place, but sadly it did, and similar incidents continued to take place pre- and post-operation while Lucia had her NG tube. I am not sure why the lady thought Alison was a single mum on benefits who went with different men who were taking drugs; maybe it was the T-shirt she wore that day that gave it away! I wish I could understand the ignorance of that lady and why she felt she had to be so rude about someone who was different. Maybe she was scared. All I know is that behaviour and attitude is not productive and helps no one.

I will say that we did not only have negative incidents with Lucia; we had a few positives ones as well. A mum asked when I was out with Lucia if her son could look at Lucia and ask about the NG tube. I sat Lucia on my lap and the little boy asked about it and was very curious and it was amazing to see his eyes light up when he was told about her heart. I think the mum was very sad and close to crying hearing about Lucia's condition, but it was a lovely conversation with them and Alison has had similar ones with others, both friends and strangers. Children are the next generation and I believe that it is our role to teach the next generation how to be more open-minded, inclusive, and understanding of others around us. You might not follow or even understand someone else's religion, for example, but that is no reason to not accept their choice of religion. The world is a massive and amazing place with lots of differences, and learning about those can only be a good thing, I think.

Two weeks had passed. The funeral was set for a couple of days after Lucia's operation. Alison was not going to go to the funeral as Lucia would more than likely still be in the Children's Intensive Care Unit (C-ICU) so she had chosen to not attend. Everyone understood.

The night before the operation, Alison took Lucia up and I stayed at home with Anabella. Lucia was put in a ward and a special gown put on her. It was so big that she looked like a doll. They put a cannula into Lucia's leg. This was in the event that they needed to administer any medicine. It could also be used by the anaesthetist to put her to sleep if need be. Alison had to sign consent forms about the operation and what they were going to do. The risks were there in black and white, clear wording saying that the operation was risky and that due to Lucia's condition there was a high probability that she could die during the surgery. She could also have serious side-effects: her heart might not function correctly and she could die post-operation.

We knew Doctor Rigby was seriously concerned about Lucia's heart. He implied that if we did not do the surgery she was at high risk of heart failure due to the stress being placed upon it. Whatever we chose to do, then, there was a risk of Lucia dying. Alison said that when she was reading the form all the noise from the ward disappeared. The words that the nurse was explaining turned to a whisper and then silence. She just stared at the form and re-read the sentence over and over again. There is a high risk and high probability that the patient could die during the operation or develop complications post-operation that could cause death.

Alison said she slept very little that night, lying in the ward next to Lucia. She did not want to leave her, but eventually she went across the road to the parent housing and went to sleep in her assigned room. Her room was at the top of the three-storey building, a very small square room. One wall had a bed against it, with a wardrobe next to it. Opposite was the little bathroom with a toilet and a shower. Near the end of the bed there was a cabinet up against the wall with a window above the cabinet. Alison used to open the window wide and climb out as it led to a small narrow roof terrace. She used to sit out there in the early hours of the morning and think about Lucia or have a cigarette. (Hopefully no one from the hospital will mind if they read this!)

On the morning of the operation, Alison wakes up after a few hours' sleep and goes over to the ward. They wake Lucia up and they cover her cannula with a plastic glove. The nurse gives Alison antiseptic soap which she uses to scrub Lucia from head to toe in a giant bath. Alison had to use it herself for her arms all the way up past her elbows. Once she was all clean, Alison was given a special gown that she had to wear to allow her to carry Lucia to make sure she did not get her dirty. Then they waited. If you have ever had an operation in a hospital, you will know that there is a lot of waiting around. It's a bit like the army: lots of training, lots of making ready, and then a lot of waiting around. Special Forces say that a lot of time they get to an incident and wait around and then it is cancelled and they pack up and go home. This day ended the same way as one of those Special Forces incidents.

After nearly an hour waiting, Lucia was due to go down. Then the nurse came and informed Alison that due to two emergency surgeries Lucia's operation has been cancelled. They had decided to cancel because Lucia had had no milk since 2 a.m. as she was unable to have anything four hours before surgery. They deemed that it would be unfair and potentially dangerous for her to not eat all day – they were not sure when in the afternoon she could have had her surgery.

Alison fed Lucia while sitting on the ward waiting for the discharge papers and the new operation date. They would not let Lucia leave unless she had her date to return. Alison gave me a call and told me what had happened, so I said that I would leave now as I was planning on coming up just before lunch after dropping Anabella off with her babysitter. The paperwork was completed, and we were giving a new operation date for the same day and time next week. I arrived, picked up all the bags and we all drove home. We waited another week.

Due to the cancelled operation, Alison was able to go to the funeral of her nan. She did not want to miss her funeral as she was very close to her nan. Aside from the funeral, the NG tube came out more often, and we went back and forth between Mayday and home getting a nurse to put it back in, and ordering more milk and syringes and tubes. One of the times I remember is Alison telling me when I got home from work that she had been to Mayday at least four times that day, as Lucia had worked out how to pull the tube out and was awake more and uncomfortable. She also seemed to be sneezing more, which was also causing the NG tube to come out. I got home and that night she pulled it out and I managed to put it all the way back in. I think that was only the second time I managed it. The next time she did it that same night, I ended up driving to Mayday hospital after midnight, having struggled to put it in. When I got to the hospital, there were a few situations happening, so I sat around the ward and waited until a nurse was free. When one was available, they also struggled to get the tube in, but in the end they managed to do it and I took Lucia home. I put her to bed and then got a few hours' sleep myself before being up and into work early.

The next operation date arrived, and the night before was the same as the previous week. Alison did not sleep very well that night either, although luckily, she was put on the top floor again, so she still had her window terrace to climb out onto if she wanted.

The following morning, the same routine took place. Lucia had a bath with antiseptic soap, Alison scrubbed her and wore the special gown which allowed her to carry Lucia. The gown on Lucia was still double the size of her. This time everything worked to plan. Alison carried Lucia down to the pre-op room. The anaesthetist told Alison to sit on a chair and hold Lucia like she was going to breastfeed her. He then gave Alison a mask to cover Lucia's nose and mouth. They said that she might fight a little and cry when they turned the gas on, but she had to keep the mask over her mouth tight. Alison would know if it was working as Lucia would get heavy when she was asleep. Alison had the mask and placed it over her nose and mouth. The gas was turned on and it started to flow. Alison got ready to hold Lucia tighter when she started to fight and cry. But it never happened. Three seconds later, Lucia was fast asleep, extremely heavy and not a sound or movement out of her. Alison placed her on the bed and then looked at her lying there still, wondering if this would be the last time that she would see her alive. She squeezed her little fingers and gave her a kiss on her forehead and then walked out of the room.

Alison described it as being on autopilot. She walked out and just stood there. She had followed all the instructions given to her by nurses, doctors and other healthcare professionals. She had no real emotions at this stage. While standing there after walking out of the pre-op room, she realised that she did not exactly know what to do next. The autopilot had only been programmed to deliver Lucia for the operation. Nothing was scheduled for during it or afterwards. She looked at the nurse that had followed her out, for guidance, the next instruction. She was standing there with a tissue in her hand. She looked at Alison and said that normally this is the part where she is giving parents cuddles and tissues and trying to calm them down as they are crying. Alison just looked at her and then around the room and took one look back at the doors behind which Lucia lay asleep.

She looked back at the nurse and said that the stage would arrive when she came off autopilot.

It was not long after this that the nurse said she should go up to the ward and wait for news there. Alison went up, packed some of the things on the bed, and gave me a quick call to find out where I was. I said I was not far away and that I would be there shortly. Alison told the nurses that she could not stay in the hospital while the operation was going on. She provided them with her mobile and my mobile just in case. The nurses said that they would call us when they were told any news and we could come back to the hospital at that point. Alison then went outside and sat on a bench with a can of red bull and her cigarettes, waiting for me to arrive.

Alison spoke to her mum to say that Lucia had been put down and the operation was going ahead and was expected to last around four hours. Her parents were flying to America that day and offered to look after Anabella so we could stay at the hospital, but we said we would be okay and that there was nothing they could do – nothing anyone could do for Lucia now, apart from her surgeons. There was no point in Alison's parents missing out on their holiday. Her mum did say that she would not buy anything for Lucia while she was away; everyone deals with situations in different ways and this was Patsy's way of dealing with Lucia's operation.

I arrived at the hospital, parked the car and could see Alison sitting on the bench with her book. I am not even sure that she was even reading the words on the page. When she looked up and saw me, the autopilot broke. The wall that was holding all of those emotions in check cracked and tumbled down quicker than a house of cards. She looked up at me and the tears appeared almost instantly. She stood up and hugged me and burst into tears, soft slow crying which slowly increased as time went by. Lots of people had to pass us to walk through the hospital doors: patients, relatives and doctors and nurses, all watching Alison crying and holding on to me. I felt like I had to hold her as tight as possible, as if I let go of her she would collapse and never get up again. I imagined that the majority of people walking past thought the worst: that our child or someone we knew had passed away.

We decided to leave the hospital and we ended up just walking around Fulham, doing everything and anything to stop us from sitting around waiting for the phone call telling us to come back to the hospital. We had coffee and lunch to pass the time. I do not remember eating, and I am not sure if I was hungry beforehand or even felt full afterwards either. We looked around the shops and we ended up buying pointless stuff, which was Alison's way of taking her mind off things. One of the things we ended up buying was a handbag from a Snappy Snaps shop which you could put a picture on. We had a picture of Anabella holding Lucia and leaning over giving her a kiss on her cheek. Such a cute picture, so we got this bag. It is one of the few pictures we have of Lucia in which she does not have the tube in her nose. We still have it; now the girls use it to play with.

Five hours later, the phone rang. This time it was the hospital. They told us that surgery has been completed and that we should come back. We turned around straightaway and headed back to the hospital without stopping. We arrived back at the C-ICU and when we got there we were told to go into a room off to the side. We turned and opened the door; there was a sign attached to the large wooden door which said 'family room'. I closed the door and turned around. Alison was already sitting in the chair and she had started to cry again. I looked around the room and saw leaflets about bereavement services and funeral directors. I sat down next to Alison and now I understood why she was crying so much. I had never been in a place like this. I have never been told to come to a hospital to visit someone before the end. This was the place where Alison and her family were put when she was told that her nan had passed away.

Alison started to scream and cry even more hysterically, saying that her baby was dead. I was unsure what to say. I just needed to do what I had done four hours earlier. I held her tight and let her cry. I was in shock, I did not want to believe that Lucia was dead and that I was just waiting to be told that the next time I saw my child she would be lying stiff and cold on the bed. I sat there next to Alison in the chair, not moving, feeling no emotions, just numb, but steady enough to hold Alison next to me.

Slowly the door opened and a nurse came in. Alison did not hear the door above her crying, but I did. I spun around. Alison felt my movement and slowly looked round at the door. The nurse just looked at us, waiting for Alison to settle down. Alison stopped crying and stood up. The nurse said that Lucia was now in her bed and comfortable. She was waiting for us. Alison smiled and looked at me and then back at the nurse, a sort of 'Did she really say that!' look. She looked back at the nurse with an expression that said 'Say that again, did I hear that right?' The nurse smiled and nodded. 'Follow me,' she said, and opened the door fully. Alison pretty much sprinted out of the room. Over that short distance, she would have given Usain Bolt a challenge.

We left the family room with the nurse leading the way and Alison closely behind. We arrived in the C-ICU area and there was Lucia lying in the middle of a bed. She was on a cooling mat which kept her core temperature down to reduce any brain or organ issues while still sedated. She looked even smaller than I remembered. There were no sides on the bed as this would get in the way of all the tubes attached to her. She had a stat machine on one side with a clip over her foot and another one for her finger. There were two large stands each containing four large syringes with various coloured liquids in each. I am not sure what all of them were. I remember that one was morphine, one was used to feed her milk, and one was another painkiller medicine. Two were to help her fight off any infections after the surgery. One was the sedation medicine. Then there were other machines. A pacemaker for her heart. Lucia had tubes coming out of her chest, her neck, two from her stomach, and tubes and needles in her arms and the backs of her hands. She was wearing just a nappy; even this looked massive on her. Like the garb of a sumo wrestler, twice the size it needed to be. She had tubes carrying oxygen into her nose and a massive plaster covering her chest, with the wires showing at the bottom of the plaster. Lucia was fast asleep and not moving, something we got used to over the next few days. I could see her chest rising and falling every so often. It seemed like every breath she took was a massive effort for her.

Alison and I looked at each other and were not sure what to do. Stay there, sit down and cry? We couldn't touch her – well, we thought we couldn't. The only part of her body which was not covered in wires or bandages was her left hand, and even then we were only able to touch three fingers. We were sitting on Lucia's left and Alison stroked the back of her fingers and then just sat down in the chair next to the bed.

She slumped down, defeated. Neither of us were sure what we were going to see when we came in, but neither of us had expected this. She looked so fragile and vulnerable. We were helpless. We could not do anything except sit there and watch. That is what we did for the rest of the day.

I asked Alison how she was feeling, and she just looked at me with no emotion again. A numb feeling. She explained later that it felt like she had taken Lucia downstairs and given her to the surgical team and they had returned with a baby that did not look like Lucia at all.

Lucia ended up staying in the C-ICU for five days before she was moved to a less critical ward.

The first two days were uneventful really. She was still heavily sedated. Alison stayed overnight in the parent block. The surgeon came round in the morning and late afternoon on both days. On the second day, he decided that he would remove the big plaster covering her chest. We were not sure exactly what her chest was going to look like underneath. We expected a large scar, very vivid. A large medical scar, red and sore. However, it was the complete opposite. The scar was clean, almost pure white in colour. Extremely straight and thin. Very neat. Alison joked with the doctor, saying that with stitching like that he could make us some new curtains. It was very impressive. Now, nearly ten years later, it is still minimal, only visible because the scar is pure white against her skin tone. The first days consisted of Alison mainly sitting in a large dull-green high-backed leather chair next to Lucia in the C-ICU. She read magazine after magazine and was told by the nurses to get food now and then, or sent to bed when she was tired. Alison remembers eating rarely. She knows she was sent away by the nurses to the canteen. She remembers ordering and paying for food and sitting at the table with her dinner in front of her. But she does not remember eating it. She had no appetite.

She would regularly fall asleep in the chair with magazine over her, as her sleep pattern was hit-and-miss. She would wake up in the early hours of the morning, like having jetlag, and go back to the C-ICU and sit next to Lucia, holding her little finger at two in the morning. There are no set visiting hours for a parent in the C-ICU. You could stay there all day and night if you wished. However, the nurses would encourage you to get rest and food. Alison's day was either sitting in the chair or sleeping, regardless of the time. She would go to sleep at 11 a.m. for a few hours, and then be back in the chair just sitting there and waiting.

The nurses gave Alison jobs to do, which Alison was more than happy with. There is nothing more depressing then sitting there watching your child and knowing you cannot do anything. The jobs were small, but they had a hugely positive impact. One was to keep Lucia's lips wet, to stop them drying out and getting sore. This would be done by getting little sticks with small pink sponges on the end. She would be given sterilised water to use. You dipped the sponge into the water and then rubbed it over Lucia's lips while she lay on the bed. You would also do it over her eyelids. As she was not opening them and blinking there was no natural moisture, so Alison needed to clean the gunk that would build up, and ensure that her eyes did not get sore.

During the course of the day the nurses would explain to her exactly what they were doing, what medicine they were giving Lucia, and why. What they were checking for, and why, and how the results compared to the last time they checked and what that meant. The nurses explained what the SAT monitor was reporting back to them. Over the course of these days in the C-ICU Alison became an expert at reading the monitor and understanding what meant what and what was happening, and most importantly, what needed to happen next. Alison admits that during the time Lucia was in C-ICU she felt very disconnected from her, not being able to pick her up, give her a cuddle or even see her awake. All we could do was touch her left hand, and to be honest that was difficult because of the tubes. The only thing not wrapped in tubes was her little finger.

It is also very difficult when you sit there hour after hour for two days with no change, and three other babies who had similar operations have already left the following day with their parents holding their child. We were unable to do it, and it was very painful. Alison spoke to her mum at some point during the second day and we explained that nothing had happened since the operation. Alison explained that, while other babies had left, her baby was still lying on the bed hooked up to machines, wires and tubes. Her mum explained that she would not be buying anything for Lucia yet as we still did not know if she would survive. That is hard to process: sitting there next to her knowing that at any point she could wake up or not wake up and that this could be your final moment with her.

I came to the hospital every morning after dropping Anabella off, either at her babysitter's, or with someone else who had offered to look after her while Lucia was in hospital. When I got to the ward, I would ask the nurse how long Alison had been there and if she has eaten anything aside from crisps and bottles of Coke or cans of Red Bull. Most of the time they would say no, and that she has been there since the early hours of the morning. I would send Alison away to get some sleep; normally I had brought her some McDonald's or something to eat. Not exactly a healthy breakfast, but better than nothing.

I would then spend a few hours sitting in the chair, reading a book and just waiting. I would look at Lucia and hold her little finger for a bit, but most of the time I would just sit there and read. The nurses did not really speak to me like they did to Alison. People have commented that the nurses focused on Alison because she was the mother. I disagree. I think they did not talk to me as much because I did not feel disconnected from Lucia. I was there, I was engaged with the nurses, and I had my snacks and drinks in the room while reading. I did not tend to worry much as I knew I could not change anything.

On the second day, I told Alison that she should go home, and I would stay overnight. She refused and shook her head furiously, as if to ask me how she could leave Lucia for even a second. I stood my ground and said that she could do nothing here and that we had another daughter, Anabella. 'She does not understand what is going on and she wants to see her mum,' I said. I explained that I understood that she felt that she must stay, but that it did not matter which one of us stayed. Eventually she agreed. I would like to say that the conversation was as civil as I have just described, but it wasn't. It was not a heated argument, but Alison believed that Lucia was poorly because of her. Therefore she felt guilty about leaving, and kept asking, what if something happened, and she was not there? She said that she would only go home for one night, and when she came back the next day she would be staying overnight again. I agreed, or else I reckon she would not have gone home that night. One night at home is better than none.

I went to get myself some food and things for the 'night shift', as I called it. Alison was still not hungry, but I was hoping that when she got home she might make herself something. I am not sure if she did eat, but I know that she slept all night. She arrived at the hospital in the early hours of the next afternoon and told me that she woke up late and had a good sleep. Objective met.

Before Alison left that night, she had to explain to me what happens during the night. She told me about the SAT machine and where the sticks and sterilised water were for the morning and during the night if need be. She took me to the parents' room where there were hot drinks and a microwave for heating food, etc. when the canteen was closed. She told me that you couldn't bring hot drinks into the ward, only cold drinks, and they must have lids. That was fine by me, I had my blackcurrant squash and water, so I was fine. She went into a lot more things, and I must admit I did not remember everything she explained. I think she was trying to make it sound complicated so that she could justify staying. But I knew that if anything serious was needed, the nurses and doctors would not be asking me to do it. They would be sending me away and getting on with it. I put my faith in the hospital and the nurses and doctors.

My evening was spent in the chair, reading my Kindle and eating snacks and drinking juice. The nurse had interrupted me at one point during the evening to ask me if I had been told about cleaning Lucia's eyes and keeping her lips wet, and I said yes. I got up and did those jobs. One stick for cleaning her eyes and another stick for her lips. I gave Lucia a little kiss on her forehead and held her finger, and I think I just looked at her and smiled at her for a while. I sat back in my chair and continued reading my Kindle until I got tired. Just after midnight I went up to the room and went to sleep and fell asleep within seconds.

I woke up just before five in the morning. I checked that my Kindle and phone were charged, and went down to the ward with my drink. I said hello to the same nurse I said goodnight to a few hours earlier. I looked at Lucia. She did not look like she had moved a millimetre since we first saw her after her operation. I spoke to the nurse again after she had done her night notes before her shift change. She explained that there had been no changes in Lucia's condition. Nothing negative has happened overnight. She had shown no improvement, but that was not a bad thing. I went back to my chair and read my Kindle until the morning rounds, when I would get a plan from the doctor. Once I had that, I would do Lucia's morning routine, cleaning her eyes and lips.

The morning of the third day and the doctor comes around. Nothing much is said and the morning is uneventful. I knew that nothing would happen for a few hours after the nurse had done her checks and taken notes, so I went and got lunch. I returned afterwards and sat back down in the chair until Alison arrived in the early hours of the afternoon. Alison explained that she slept all morning. She thanked me for it, even if she had not wanted to go originally. A few hours after Alison arrived, the doctor explained that they were going to try and bring Lucia out of sedation. To do this, he explained, they would be raising her internal body temperature. This would mean turning off the cooling sheet underneath Lucia.

An hour later they had checked their notes and planned how they would do it. The sheet was turned off or down, I am not sure which. This allowed her core temperature to slowly rise. They reduced the sedation medicine as well. As her temperature started to rise, her body and heart struggled to regulate it. After a while, some machines started beeping. Numbers started to climb. In the middle of all this, Lucia did not move a millimetre. The nurse came in and started to check the monitors. Then there was some rushing around. Doctors were called, and they looked at various machines and started changing things. Lots of medical people rushing around, and still Lucia does not move. The abnormal rhythm of her heart was dangerous, and causing stress on her heart. A heart that had only been repaired a few days ago. They put the cooling sheet back on and cooled her core body temperature down again. They increase the sedation medicine back to its original level. They also attached a pacemaker to her heart and set this to control her heart rhythm, and after a little while her heart was back to normal and she was back where she had been a few hours before. After she was settled, they turned the pacemaker off and detached the wires from her chest and placed the caps back on.

Through all of this her body had not moved. I was expecting her body to shake or her to move around with her heart beating in and out of control, fast and unbalanced – but nothing. She was still lying on her back, her head facing to the right, her left hand still close to the edge, close enough for either Alison or me to reach out from our chair and stroke her fingers like before.

After this episode, Alison refused to leave the chair. She would not leave for food or to get a drink. She got into such a panic, similar to when Lucia first went down for her operation. I think that, for the first time since Lucia got ill, Alison genuinely believed that she would not survive. So she sat in the chair and did not move. She slumped down and just looked at Lucia. She held her little finger and tried not to cry. I could see the tears slowly forming and sliding down her cheek and then onto her upper lip. I told her to go home and rest. 'There is nothing that either of us can do,' I said. She ignored me, just stared at Lucia and tried to keep fighting back the tears.

I realised that Alison was not going to move regardless of whatever I did or said, and I also knew which battles to fight and when to accept defeat and move on. This was one of the latter. I got Alison some magazines and some Coke and some snacks. Not that I expected her to eat them. I went home and picked up Anabella. I then sat on the sofa with her, watching a Disney film and just cuddled until she fell asleep in my lap.

The following morning was day four. I thought Alison needed some time alone, so I decided to spend some time with Anabella. Some Daddy-Daughter time. I took her to the park after breakfast. We played on the swings and walked around. When she got tired we came home and played card games such as Snap and Pairs. We had a lot of fun. She asked about Mummy and her little sister. Asked if she could see them, and I said I was not sure. I made her some lunch and decided to take her to the hospital. I tried to explain what was happening, but she did not understand. All she understood was that Mummy and her little sister were not at home.

Anabella and I arrived at the hospital and Anabella was like a kid in a sweetshop. She was wandering around the hospital, all excited. When we got into the ward, she saw Alison, and then spun around looking at the three beds in the large room. She walked over to Lucia's bed and looked at all the machines. I lifted her up so she could see Lucia in bed. She just looked at me and said one word and pointed towards her sister. 'Lulu.' That is all she said. I think that was when Anabella realised that Lucia was special and that her job was to look after her. Ever since then she has. Anabella and I were only at the hospital for a few hours, but enough for Alison to feel connected and interact, as opposed to being slumped alone in the chair. Any time a nurse came near Lucia, Anabella would look to see what they were doing and then check the machine afterwards. Like she was checking it was still the same. I had brought some toys and some colouring and reading books for Anabella, and we set her up to play and she was happy and focused until a nurse came by again. Then, after checking on her sister, she would return to her colouring or reading.

Alison filled me in on the events of the day, including the part when they tried to wake Lucia up again. They had tried it twice, meaning that the first time they tried on day four, the result was the same as on day three. The second time, though, they had done something different: this time they left the pacemaker attached and ensured that the machine set the pace of her heart.

Alison went back into panic mode. She sat in her chair and this time instead of just being numb she was anxious and couldn't keep still. Her hands kept moving and she kept grabbing magazines or drink bottles. Anything and everything to try and keep herself busy and her mind focused on something else. It didn't work.

They reduced Lucia's sedation again and turned off the cooling sheet underneath her. They checked the pacemaker and left it doing most of the work, and said that they would check her progress every hour or two. Lucia still had not moved a muscle. In four days, nothing. The first hour dragged. It felt like days, according to Alison, wondering when the machines were going to beep warning signals or the SAT monitor go red, with the numbers on the right-hand side rising. It did not happen. The doctors and nurses came back every hour or so and checked machines. The pacemaker machine was the one that seemed to get the most attention; it was regulating her heart at a pre-set pace to try and ensure that her heart did not fail or become erratic like before. Luckily it was working, according to all the machines that were attached to her.

After a while, the doctors and nurses were happy and felt that Lucia was comfortable. The pacemaker was doing its job. Her heart was steady and not abnormal. Her core temperature was also higher, so her internal organs could start to function, and she was having no adverse reaction to the rise. They had also increased the morphine slightly after one of the checks. Not sure what they had seen, but something must have indicated to them that she was in pain (or reacting to pain).

The best news was that because the nurses and doctors were happy and felt Lucia was stable at this point, they decided to change her bedding and allow Alison to hold her. Alison loved this thought. She felt like she was going to be able to hold our baby girl. Unfortunately, it was not that simple.

Because of all the tubes and the fact of her open-heart surgery, what they did was get Alison to sit in the chair but really close to the bed this time. They told Alison to put her arms out, and Alison thought she was going to hold Lucia. But no: they gave her a pillow which was placed across her arms and on her lap. The nurses lifted Lucia out of the bed very careful and placed her onto the pillow. It was very slow, moving her, very steady; it would be dangerous to tilt her, and the nurses could not pick her up under her arms, as that would put undue pressure on her heart. So Alison was sitting in the chair cuddling a pillow, but she would not be able to physically touch her. There were still lots of wires hanging over the bed and across Alison's shoulders attached to Lucia. So, in short, Alison got to cuddle a pillow. Not for very long either. Because of the stress of being on a pillow and being moved, the nurses were very quick to change the bedding. It was a total of five minutes to change the bed and then put Lucia back. Alison said it felt like five seconds. She felt that they had just put her on her lap and then seconds later put her back. She felt useless again. The knowledge that she was unable to lean forward to give her a cuddle or a light hug or even a kiss on her forehead because you might end up doing more harm to her was awful. If her body was not straight and therefore put the tiniest bit of pressure on her heart, it could be enough to could kill her. Shortly after they had put Lucia back, Anabella and I arrived.

Anabella wanted to climb onto the bed and see Lulu, but we couldn't let her. Too many wires, too dangerous. Anabella did not understand this, and started to play up after a little while when we kept saying no. She pointed to the wires and then to Lucia. She said that they were to make her better, and at one point asked Lucia to wake up.

During the course of that afternoon, the doctors' and nurses' visits were more frequent. In the afternoon they told us that they would be reducing the work being done by the pacemaker over the course of twenty-four hours. It was important that her heart was pumping and regulating her body by itself. So they spent time looking at the settings and making some kind of plan about how much to reduce it and over what length of time until eventually the machine could be switched off. I think it ended up being every three or four hours that they would come in and review the situation.

When Anabella got tired, I took her home and again we sat on the sofa watching a film or TV show that she wanted to watch. I was not focusing on the TV, so it did not make any difference to me; then I put her to bed. I felt extremely tired, but I think that night was the first time I felt hopeful after how Lucia reacted being woken. She may not have moved, but her heart had remained steady and they were making her heart work by itself. Tomorrow morning would be critical to see how she had coped overnight, and I went to sleep trying to encourage the morning to arrive sooner.

The following morning, I woke up early, Anabella was going to stay with friends for the weekend, so I could be at the hospital all day and the majority of the night if I wanted. I dropped Anabella off after breakfast and she was excited but asked when Mummy and Lulu were coming home. I believed that Lucia was coming home that morning, but I got down on my knees and picked up Anabella and gave her a big cuddle and said that I didn't know when they were coming home – hopefully soon – and gave her a kiss. She told me to give kisses to Mummy and Lulu from her, and then went back to the toys and books that she had brought with her.

I arrived at the hospital and Alison was sitting in the chair. I suspected that she had been there all night, or at least the majority of it. She turned her head and I could see that she was smiling. She had energy. She was not slumped in the chair. She had been there all night, but she had been happy about it as opposed to worried. She got out of the chair and said that she was starving for breakfast, and could we go and get something. We checked with the nurse when the rounds were due and if anything was due to happen for the next hour, and there was nothing. The last pacemaker adjustment had only been done an hour ago, so nothing more would happen until the doctor completed his morning rounds. We knew from experience that we had at least two hours before he would be in our room.

We headed to the canteen and sat down, and both had a good big breakfast. Alison had more than dry toast, so I knew she was feeling better. Physically, she was exhausted, but I thought that maybe I could convince her to go home that night and get some rest. Alison told me how Lucia was doing. Everything was being reduced slowly, and she had not reacted at all, which was good. She thought that they would stop the sedation completely today, and maybe the morphine would be reduced again; we would know more following the morning rounds.

Day five, and our baby could be waking up properly and some of the wires and tubes be removed. This could be a very good day. After the last four days, we needed this. The doctor did his morning rounds and explained the next steps. Alison was spot on. They were going to stop her sedation shortly, and after that they were going to stop her pacemaker as well. They were also going to stop the other medicine and reduce the morphine to a low dose, depending on how she reacted. So it was going to be a full-on day. They did flag up that they were concerned that her heart was still very weak, so the situation was still very dangerous. We took it as a make-or-break situation.

We got ready for a long day ahead. I took a chair from beside an empty bed and we set up our chairs and snacks. My Kindle was fully charged, and I had enough books to keep me going, and so I settled into my chair ready to read.

During the morning and early afternoon, Lucia's medicines were reduced or stopped, her pacemaker was reduced, and everyone was watching her for reactions; it seems like every hour someone was writing notes and checking charts. Adjustments were made to the syringes and other machines. It seemed that everything was going to plan. They were no changes that I could see, and there was nothing in the doctors' and nurses' reactions that gave us any cause for concern.

Early evening, just before the doctor left for the night, I thought of something and called him back. I explained that I thought the pacemaker was being turned off today. He said that this had been the plan in the morning; however, some of her reactions to the reducing of the medicines had made him revise that plan and keep the pacemaker on. He had stopped all the medicines though. He was expecting her to react tomorrow morning and show signs of movement, which made us both smile.

So the end of day five saw Lucia on no medication. No IV injections, morphine, and no sedation. Just her pacemaker, attached to her heart keeping it steady. That was a good night.

Day six. This was another good day. Lucia woke up properly and moved around. The doctor came around and was happy with everything. He said that we would now stop the pacemaker to see how she was for the morning, and if he was happy then the wires would be removed as well.

Everything worked according to plan. Lucia did not react with the pacemaker off. However, before they decided to remove the wires they moved Lucia out of C-ICU to a low-dependency ward. The room was similar in size. A C-ICU room consists of four beds in a room with eight nurses, hence a nurse-to-child ratio of 2:1. Low-dependency wards are not as serious as ICU but need more attention than a regular ward; here, the ratio is 1:1. I decided to go back and get Anabella, knowing that she wanted to see her sister when she woke up. Anabella and I returned just as Alison had finished cleaning her eyes and wetting her lips. She was playing with her a little. We were still unable to pick her up or touch her really, with the pacemaker wires still in her heart. Anabella was so excited to see her little sister opening her eyes that she tried to climb onto the bed with her, just as she had when Lucia was first admitted to Mayday. At Mayday it was fine, as the bed was like a prison cell, tall bars all the way up so neither child could fall off – plus Lucia had no wires in her or around her then. This time was different. Most of the wires and tubes had gone, but there were still a couple. We moved the wires and let Anabella sit at the end of the bed by Lucia's feet where there was a space. She just sat there playing with an iPad or reading a book, with the occasional glance over to Lucia to check that she was still there. She asked for a cuddle with Lucia and the nurse said that she could, as long as we were there, and we held Anabella up so she did not put her weight on Lucia. I laid her across my arms and then she leaned over and gave Lucia a little cuddle. She was so excited being able to cuddle her sister.

Later in the afternoon, two things happened. One: Lucia stirred and wriggled around and moved a little. There was no sound from her, a little moan maybe, but no crying. This made all three of us happy, especially Anabella, who was still sitting on the end of the bed when it happened. The second was that the doctor returned, saying that they were going to remove the wires from the pacemaker now. The pacemaker had not been on and her heart had been managing fine on its own. This would not be pleasant for Lucia as it would hurt, but there was no risk that something could go wrong.

The doctor moved some wires around and then undid the tape holding the wires to her chest. They removed the pacemaker machine so there was more room around the bed. Then the doctor started to pull the wires out slowly from her chest. At this point, Lucia screamed. She was screaming and crying a lot. This was the first time in five months that we had heard her cry. Alison was getting upset, and left the room, taking Anabella with her, until it was all over. I stayed and just stood to the side of the bed where there was room, holding her left hand and waiting.

This was another moment when time seemed distorted, as it felt like ages that I was standing there listening to her cry while unable to do anything. In fact, I do not think it lasted more than thirty seconds from when the doctor started pulling the wires out to his walking out of the room. Alison and Anabella came back in and Lucia was still crying a little, though not as much as before. The nurse was happy that we could do the NG properly. The nurse was tense and anxious but not in a bad way. It was like she was getting ready to react if and when, as opposed to having to stop something. Like a runner on the starter blocks. Waiting for the gun to be fired. She was waiting for something to go wrong, and when she realised that she would not be needed, she relaxed. It felt good to be feeding Lucia and having only the SAT machine there and her NG tube in place.

Alison was feeling a lot better. The whole week had mentally and physically drained her more than I realised. She was a lot happier with all the wires and tubes gone, but she was still running on empty. Just pure adrenaline. I discussed the idea that maybe she should take Anabella home and rest at home again. Lucia was getting better and the worst was now over, and Alison needed to catch up on sleep and eat properly, which you can never do really in a hospital. Anabella overheard and smiled lots, saying that she would get Mummy time and watch a film on the sofa with her like she did with me. I think Alison was tempted to say no; that she should stay. But Anabella looked so happy at the thought of having Mummy time that she could not say no. Anabella to the rescue. They both went home in the early hours of the evening and I settled down for a long evening sitting in the chair, drinking juice and reading my Kindle as usual. I moved the chair into a good position, where I could see Lucia if she woke up and was able to stroke her hand if she stirred. I got all the milk and water equipment ready, as I would need to feed her every four hours.

A couple of hours in, the nurse informed me that we were going to move Lucia to main ward. She was no longer classed as low dependency, now her pacemaker wires had been removed and her vitals had been stable all afternoon. I got everything packed up after having it laid out a few hours earlier. They moved her bed out of the room and around the corner, into a larger room off to the side. A main ward room is a lot larger, as the nurse ratio is very different.

The ratio here was 1:4, so one nurse for four children. The room held eight beds. A children's ward generally requires a nurse to be always present in the room, so we had one nurse at the end of the room with her paperwork, checking on all eight of us, and the other nurse would be getting equipment and such things. They swapped around every few hours but there was always a nurse available if we needed them.

I got my chair and the other things ready again. Lucia had started to stir, and I checked with the nurse when her last feed was, to see if that was what was needed. It was. I did all the checks and fed her without any issues. Lucia was awake then, so I played with her a little bit. I was not sure if I could pick her up at that point; I did not ask, as suspected that a nurse would tell me if I could. I just read her a story and gave her a soft toy of some description. She was happy for a little while and then fell asleep and I went back to my chair.

The night was uneventful. I went to bed late and woke up early and spent my time reading and feeding Lucia. It was a nice relaxed evening. The nurse explained that any medicine would also be put down her NG tube now. The morning arrived, and the nurse said that we could now do all the normal things such as changing nappies, etc., and we could pick her up as well. That was the best news ever. The nurse explained that we could not pick her up under her arms as you would normally because of the surgery. We had to scoop her up like a shovel, one hand under her bum and up her back, and support the back of her neck. She said we should also try and keep her lying on her back and not lift her vertically yet. That meant there would not be any undue stress on her heart.

The morning of day seven. We had been at the hospital for a week. The morning was all about medicine down the NG tube, post-operation care with the sponges, cleaning her eyes and lips, and changing her nappy, which the nurses weighed to check how much is coming out compared to Lucia's intake of milk and water. And most importantly cuddles. Lots of cuddles when she was awake. Lucia was still very tiny and fragile. She looked like a new-born baby that had been delivered premature. She was five months old.

Alison arrived in the afternoon without Anabella and we spoke to the nurse and asked if they had any issues with us leaving the hospital together for dinner after we had done the feeding, etc. The nurses were fine with it. They said that we had been there longer than most and it would be fine. We left after the early-evening feed, having cleaned her and changed her. Lucia was asleep. We left the hospital and went for a walk in the evening air. It was September, but not cold and windy, a nice cool calm night for a walk. We began to relax a little, and I think we were okay for the first thirty, maybe forty, minutes. Alison then wanted to get back. Dinner was not a proper dinner in a restaurant, but something hot which filled a hole. We got back to the hospital and went back up to the ward. Lucia had not moved, and the nurse was a little surprised to see us back so soon. We had only been gone an hour, but it was an hour that we both needed.

I left shortly after that and just missed the evening rounds. The doctor advised Alison that potentially we could be going home tomorrow if the evening was uneventful and the morning was the same. He said that they had no worries; that he had no reason to keep us in. Alison can't remember whether she jumped up and hugged the doctor or not. But she slept better that night, knowing that Lucia could be coming home the following day. It felt like a huge weight had been lifted off her shoulders.

She called me later than night after I had put Anabella to bed. She told me what the doctor had said. I made arrangements for someone to have Anabella while we were signing out, and said that I would come up late morning, as nothing would get confirmed until after the morning rounds.

It was the morning of day eight since the operation. The morning we were bringing Lucia home. I got everything sorted and arrived at the hospital around 10:30. The doctor was walking out of the room just as I got there. I expected they would make their decision during morning rounds and then take a few hours to get all the paperwork and medicines/milk together. We would leave just after lunch and get some dinner on the way back, or have a take-out when we got home.

The morning routine had been the same as yesterday: no issues from the nurses overnight, and nothing extra from the doctor during his rounds. The nurses were sorting out some special milk called Infantrini, a high-calorie milk which would help increase Lucia's weight and give her all the things she needed. I had brought some NG tubes from home to check, as the equipment might be different. It was, and they spent some time matching equipment to the tubes we had. We did not need any syringes or sponges as we still had a lot from Croydon.

We sat around waiting, packed up the majority of her things, and I started taking some of the bigger bags containing clothes downstairs to the car. In the end we sat there for about an hour with just Lucia and a small bag of snacks, waiting.

After lunch, the nurse arrived and told us we could take our little girl home. We were so excited. We said goodbye to all the nurses and some of the other parents. We were used to others saying goodbye to us, so it was nice to be doing it the other way around.

We left and climbed into the car and drove home to West Norwood. I would like to say that after that it was all good; but it was not. Alison's parents invited us over to Gibraltar for a holiday, which was amazingly thoughtful. We needed two weeks away in the sunshine with both our girls and just relax. The issue was all the medical equipment that we would need to bring, as well as the milk; this was after the 9/11 attacks on the Twin Towers in New York, and you were not allowed to carry any liquid over 100ml. Lucia's milk was double this, and was provided direct by the NHS. It was also sterile, so we were unable to open it and then use it later.

In fact, flying out with BA and through Gatwick, the service was fantastic. We explained the situation and we had letters from Broomfield on NHS-headed paper explaining what operation she had had and the purpose of the tube and the special milk. We also had a special pushchair in which Lucia lay flat to relieve the stress on her heart. We would have to use it all the way to door of the plane. The airline understood, and explained to security. I had to show the paperwork multiple times, but there were no issues. They checked and verified what we said and allowed us to take the pushchair to the door of the plane. In the end, the captain came out and spoke to us. He allowed our pushchair to be placed in his special area where his things went, so that we would not have to wait when we landed for the pushchair to be offloaded and delivered to the gate.

That was amazing, and the flight went very well. Both children were very well behaved until landing, when Lucia cried with the change in pressure; but it was not for long, and after not hearing that sound for so long until last week, I was glad that she was crying. The two weeks in the sun were excellent and just want we needed.

Then came the time to come home. This did not go so well.

The problem was the Gibraltar security people when we were

getting on the plane. They took the medical box without an issue; the issue was the milk coming onto the flight. They were shown the letters and the explanations – that Lucia had a genetic disorder and had had open heart surgery only a month ago. But they were not that interested. The woman security guard was the most difficult about the milk. I was required to open half of what I wanted to take with us. And she wanted me to drink from half the bottles before they allowed us to board the plane.

I kept explaining that it was sterile milk and that once I open it, it would be useless: we could not use it later. She shrugged like it was not her problem. I demanded to see a supervisor, to which she replied she was the supervisor. I asked for her boss and was told that they were busy and that I was holding up the line. The quicker I drank the milk, the quicker we can board, they said. I was not interested in the line being held up behind me, I was interested in my daughter and could not believe that I was being told that her medical problems were not of any interest to these people.

After at least twenty minutes of conversations that were getting heated, including the threat that I would not be allowed on the plane and that the flight would be cancelled, I open three of the milk bottles and drank some of the milk. It was horrible. It tasted like warm milk, which is not very nice at all. If you haven't tried it, then save your taste buds that experience. I left the bottles at the security desk and was told that I had to put the lids on them and take them with me. I point blank refused to do that. I explained that they were now useless as medical milk, as explained in all the documentation I had with me. I turned and walked away with my family and we boarded the plane.

Lucia had two of the remaining bottles and slept more on the way back than she did on the way to Gibraltar, so it was okay. However, I do not think that it should have been this difficult. Knowing that there are other parents who have children with even more complex needs than Lucia, I can only imagine the struggle that they must go through any time they board an aircraft. I can also understand why several parents I know choose not to go on holiday abroad and stay in the UK, as it is a lot easier.

15 – HOSPITAL OPERATIONS: MULTIPLE PALATE OPERATIONS

The biggest issue that Lucia has had to deal with so far is her palate. She has had to have four operations so far, all under general anaesthetic. She has one final operation remaining, which is due to take place in October 2018. Three of these operations have been to correct her palate and each one has had a measure of success. One of the operations was purely to remove her tonsils. There was nothing wrong with them, they just needed to be removed as it was deemed that they were too big and were in the way for one of the other operations.

Lucia was in her final year of pre-school nursery. The speech therapist advised that she was not making the sounds that she should be, and the airflow when making sounds was not correct. She spoke to the doctors and prepared us for the idea that they would recommend surgery to correct her palate. We spoke to the doctors and they explained what they thought was the issue and that they would be doing some tests to check, and then confirm what they needed to do.

Over the course of four months, Lucia had several tests. One of the major ones that took place was an x-ray of her palate. The speech therapist spoke to us about what this would entail. Lucia would speak into a microphone attached to an x-ray machine, while looking into a kid's toy. The toy was a pair of glasses with pictures inside. The x-ray machine did not just take pictures, it was video as well. It would record Lucia talking.

We arrived at the hospital and Anne, her speech therapist, took us into the room and explained what they were aiming to do. The room was a standard hospital room, where Lucia had her speech therapy. Anne explained in a little more detail what was due to happen and what she suspected were Lucia's issues and the likely outcome. She explained that the palate has two areas that must meet to allow the airflow to either go out of her nose or not. So the roof of the palate is like the barrier. This is called the hard palate. This part contains bone. The soft palate is just muscle.

The hard palate is fixed. It is solid and does not move and is located at the back of your mouth and the roof of your mouth, like a back wall of your garden. The soft palate is located at the front of your mouth and moves to control and direct the airflow. Imagine the soft palate being like a door. So the door swings up and down in the mouth, controlling airflow. To stop air coming out of your nose, the door (soft palate) goes up and hits the barrier (hard palate) and therefore the air comes out of your mouth. When you make the sound of the letter 't' the soft palate moves up against the hard palate, stopping the airflow which allows you to make the 't' sound out of your mouth.

In the case of Lucia, the airflow was coming out of her nose. Therefore, she was not making the correct sounds and not developing her muscles correctly. Anne explained this to us and then took us to the x-ray room. Lucia was only four years old at the time. It was a large room with computers and video cameras on one side. These were blocked off behind a long window enclosure. The x-ray machine was large. There was a microphone attached to a pole in the middle, with the kid's eye toy just above it.

They brought Lucia in and set the microphone and the toy to her height. She was meant to stand still, look into the toy and then repeat the words which were said to her. These words and phrases would test the whole movement and development of her palate muscles. Unfortunately, she was unable to do it, even with me next to her in a heavy lead gown to protect me from the x-rays. She looked at the picture and then moved away to tell me about it. We continued to try different methods with the technicians for fifteen to twenty minutes before stopping the test. She was unable to stay still long enough or talk long enough into the microphone to capture the sounds she produced, or for the video camera to record the whole movement of her mouth.

They gave us some ideas to get her to stand still and speak as clearly as possible, and re-booked her in for six months' time. This would be when she would be in reception at school, so we explained to the school what was due to happen. The teacher knew a little sign language from her previous role working in a specialist school and would develop this with us and Lucia during her reception year.

The school still sign now with the younger children. I think it is an amazing skill for children to learn. They perform all the primary plays with signs as well as speech. The songs for the Christmas nativity are signed. Seeing nearly eighty children singing 'Rudolph The Red-Nosed Reindeer' as well as signing the actions is fantastic; I never get tired of watching it.

For six months we worked with the school and at home getting Lucia ready for the x-ray test again. We purchased a cheap toy microphone and a kaleidoscope-type toy for her. We did between thirty seconds and a minute every morning before school and when she got home after school every day. We stood still holding the toy with both hands, so she would not be tempted to move. We would hold the microphone up to her and get her to sing a song or say anything she wanted. After four months, she was able to stand still for nearly three minutes and speak for almost all that time. Three minutes may not seem a long time, but as a parent you will know that getting any child to stand still for thirty seconds is hard without an electronic device or a TV, so we were very pleased with this.

I believe it helped that we made the task as fun as possible. We turned it into a game, where I would say that I could see the picture, describe something different, and she would correct me. We would also give her a time limit and then reward her with treats if she managed it. At the beginning we broke things down into smaller tasks, such as thirty seconds, but she would turn around and talk after five seconds; we would tell her to carry on and let's get to thirty seconds, regardless of how many times she stopped. This allowed us to give her a bigger treat or reward when she managed to do it in one go. Then you start the cycle all over again, now knowing that she should be able to do, as a minimum, thirty seconds.

The next test came around very quickly. Lucia was much better this time around. She did stop occasionally and turned around, but a little encouragement and the promise of a chocolate muffin from the

M&S shop afterwards was enough to get her to do the test in full. The nurses got everything they needed and told us that we would have to wait a couple of hours while the photos and video of the test were completed and sent to the doctors for review. Our appointment for the x-ray test was scheduled for 10:30 and we ended doing our test around 11 a.m. and were done by around 11:30. We were scheduled to come back to the doctors at 3 p.m. Anabella was at school and we had booked her into after-school club, but the school were fully aware that we were at the hospital. We had friends nearby who could collect her from school if we were going to be later than when the after-school club finished at 5:30. We hoped for the best but had planned for the worst. Also, Sofia was at nursery and her grandparents were going to pick her up for us and take her back to their house. We would pass their house on the way back from the hospital and collect her on the way to school for Anabella. This was the plan.

After lunch, we sat in the waiting room at the hospital. Alison had her iPad and Kindle, I had my Kindle, and Lucia was playing with the toys we had brought and the ones from the hospital. Lucia and I played Pairs and other card games, which Lucia still loves playing to this day. She wanted cuddle time, where she would sit on my lap and rest her head into my shoulder or chest and I would read her a story or put the iPad on for her to play a game. Normally something like Pairs or simple maths games, in which she could point to the answer without moving her head.

After a while she fell asleep, so I laid her down on the long sofa in the waiting room and sat at one end, holding her so she did not fall off. I continued to read my Kindle, with the odd trip out of the waiting room to the main walkway where there was a Costa Express and a few other shops, to get something to eat and a hot chocolate.

Anne came and got us just after 3 p.m. She led us into one of the larger therapy rooms, which had a mini TV in the corner, and there were two doctors and another lady who had sorted out the administration as well as the transfer to the ward after the operation, all of them waiting for us.

The doctor showed us the video of Lucia's x-ray test. He was explaining what should be happening and the movement of the soft palate muscle and where it should be reaching at the roof of her palate. This was not happening for Lucia. Her soft palate was moving but not very much and nowhere near the roof of her mouth. He explained that he believed that they should build onto her roof and close the gap between the roof of her mouth and the soft palate muscle. Lucia was fascinated to hear her voice out of the speakers, and to see her mouth moving in black and white on the screen. The doctor continued to explain what the operation would consist of. They would take skin from the inside of her cheek and then add it to the roof of her mouth, thereby reducing the gap.

We were expecting a long delay while the operation was set. How wrong we were. He said he had a slot in two or three weeks. All palate operations there are scheduled for a Wednesday and they do three each day. Alison has her diary with her and we agreed that three weeks' time would be best.

We left the hospital just gone 3:30 and drove back to Alison's parents to tell them what was happening. They would be back from holiday then, and said that they would be happy to have Anabella and Sofia overnight at the time of the operation. I agreed that I would drop them off in the morning on my way to the hospital. Alison would be leaving early with Lucia as you have to be in hospital around 7 a.m. on operation days. Lucia would be the first operation of the day. We left to pick up Anabella from school and take her home. Anabella was curious as to how it had gone with Lucia. We gave her a summary of what was going to happen. I explained to work the next day what was happening. We were not expecting the operation to be as difficult as her heart was, but her recovery had not been easy there, and we suspected that her recovery from this operation would not be very good either.

Operation One:
The morning of the first operation. The roof of her mouth. Alison and Lucia drove down to the hospital and got there around 7 a.m. Lucia was admitted and placed in a bed on the ward. Alison got all the toys out and all the other equipment that had become part of our usual hospital bag. As part of the process, they required that Lucia have a bath in a special room in the ward. This bath was massive, surprisingly big for small children. Lucia loved it, as she could swim a few strokes in it and go underwater. A special soap was used to ensure that her whole body was clean. I was slightly taken aback by this, considering that this was a palate operation. Alison said it was

part of the process to get children calm and ready. They came and got Lucia just before 8 a.m. to go down. The anaesthetist was there and explained to Alison what they needed her to do to put her to sleep. She would hold her like a baby in her arms, then place the green balloon over her nose and mouth. They would then turn the gas on and Alison would hold her until she fell asleep. They told Alison to expect Lucia to fight a little and maybe cry but she still had to keep the balloon over her face.

Lucia did not make a sound. She fell asleep within five seconds and then Alison passed her over to the nurse. She was placed on the bed and then pushed through the big double doors into the operation theatre, where her doctor was waiting.

During all this, I had given the girls breakfast and dropped them both off at school. The nursery had been told that Sofia's grandparents would be picking her up, and the same for Anabella. (The nursery was next door to the school, so it made the trip very easy for Alison's parents.) After I had dropped them off at school, I drove straight to the hospital. I found Alison outside in the walkway by the Costa coffee stand, reading her book and waiting. When I got to her table, I could see that she was not really reading.

We waited around for a few hours, and read, talked and had coffee and snacks, until Anne came and found us. When we went back to the ward, there was Lucia lying in the middle of the bed, just as she had at the Royal Brompton Hospital after her heart operation. The difference here was that this time she just had an NG tube in her nose, no wires or other tubes. A lot easier to manage than before. She was fast asleep. The nurse explained that it would be a few hours before the anaesthetic wore off and that then they would give her Calpol and Nurofen alternately every few hours. Alison checked all the other things we had brought with us and got the area set up with the pull-out bed for her later that night. We sat next to Lucia, waiting for her to wake up. A couple of hours later, she did. She screamed once she woke up – lots of crying and screaming and not much else. She refused to eat anything, she refused to drink anything. The nurses gave her Calpol and Alison wrote it down in her book. We were told that the best way to help heal her throat would be smooth foods to soothe the place where the inside of her mouth was cut. Plenty of ice cream while it was sore, as well. She also needed to drink lots of water and her milk. The water would keep the wound clean to prevent any infections, and the milk was to maintain her weight.

The rest of the evening was a mixture of crying, screaming, cuddling, and sleeping on Alison. Alison climbed onto the bed with her and Lucia cuddled up on her chest watching the iPad, mostly Disney films, which was no bad thing as I love a good Disney film. (However, the same one six times a day I am sure would drive any Disney enthusiast slightly crazy.) Lucia slept a lot and therefore the Calpol and Nurofen were given to her through her NG tube. However, when she woke up one time she did not like the feeling of her NG tube and proceeded to pull it out. I have never had one, but I am sure it feels very uncomfortable having a tube in your nose and all the way down the back of your throat. They put it back in later that night, as Lucia still refused to eat or drink anything. A few sips here and there, but nothing substantial. Without the NG tube, Lucia would have had to take her medicine orally, and she refused. The nurses put the NG tube back in, and to stop her from pulling it out again they wrapped her hands in bandages. Lucia was not impressed.

The rest of the evening continued in the same way: they asked Lucia to eat and drink and take her medicine orally; while the tube helped in some ways, it did not help the healing process on the roof of her throat. The tube bypassed the roof of her throat and therefore food and drink did not go past it. She was told that tomorrow morning the tube would be removed, and she would have to eat and drink and take her medicine orally from then on. Lucia screwed up her face and shook her head vigorously at that suggestion, then lay down on her pillow to go to sleep. Alison got herself ready for a whole night sleep.

I had already gone home and collected the other two from their grandparents. I did not need to feed them as they had already eaten, and they had had baths and were in their pyjamas by the time I collected them. Alison's mum does so much with the girls when they have them, looking after all the little things you have to do with children, so I do not need to worry about them when I pick them up. These little things take such a huge amount of pressure off Alison and me, so we can focus on the main things, such as getting the girls ready for school and back up to the hospital and then home and to bed. Film nights on the sofa are a tradition that started due to the amount of time that Lucia has spent in hospitals; it was a way that I got to spend some time with the other girls when I had very little. We still have film night nearly every weekend, eight years later.

The first night was pretty uneventful. The nurses came every two hours and gave her medicine via her NG tube and Alison slept the majority of the evening. Occasionally Lucia would wake up crying a little and in pain, but a five-minute cuddle on the bed with Alison was enough to calm her down and send her back to sleep. At one point, Alison was woken up by the nurses to feed.

Day two: Lucia woke up crying, but not as much as the day before, which Alison took as progress. After the morning dose of medicine, the bandage-gloves were removed along with the NG tube. Lucia was not happy as she knew that she would have to eat and drink, which she said was still too painful. During the day Alison and I invented drinking games to get her to drink. (Now Lucia is ten, so in ten years' time, Lucia will playing very different drinking games, I have no doubt.) However, at three the drinking games were part of playing Pairs. We set up the cards and when she got a pair she had to have a sip of water or juice. We also said that if she won we would get her a treat like a chocolate muffin, and the play lady at the hospital said that she would bring her some painting things so she could paint in bed. Lucia loved this idea. During that day, she got ice cream in bed and even had ice cream for breakfast. We got her to drink more and more as the day wore on. She had chocolate muffins. Near the end of the day, she was drinking more and eating too, but she was still very tearful and still nowhere near eating and drinking as much she needed to before they considered her able to leave.

Alison set herself up for another night, thinking that it would be like the night before. Sadly, she was mistaken. Because Lucia was still not eating and drinking enough, the nurses needed to have her eat and drink through the night as well. So Alison was given a chart of how much water and milk she needed to have drunk over the course of the day, broken down into two-hour amounts, so we could monitor them in between her medicine, which was administered every two hours as well. This resulted in the nurses waking Alison up every two hours so she could give Lucia her medicine and liquid intake. This was then recorded, both by the nurses for their file and by Alison for her own notes.

Day three. Alison's grandparents had agreed to take Anabella and Sofia for the weekend. They would collect them both after school and then they would stay. I took them both to school in the morning and told the schools that their grandparents would be collecting them. Then I drove back to the hospital. Once I got to the hospital, I got myself a hot chocolate from the Costa stand in the main walkway and called my work and advised them that I was not sure if I would be in work the following week or working from home. They understood, and I told them that I would update them on Monday morning. A few of my colleagues who I was close with were going to message me over the coming weekend with Get Well Soon messages for Lucia, and told me not to worry about work. I am one of those lucky people who loved my job at the time. I spend all day with problems to resolve, large amounts of data and numbers to check and reconcile so as to ensure that the whole process worked from start to finish. It was all down to me to check that everything was working as it should. I finished my hot chocolate and went to see Alison and Lucia.

I arrived to find Lucia screaming that she did not want to drink her milk or any water, as it hurt. Alison was looking physically drained, and I imagined that she had been up a lot of the night. How right I was, I discovered, when we had a catch-up later when Lucia was asleep. I took over from Alison and tried to get Lucia to drink while Alison went and had a walk and calmed down. Lucia got worse. She screamed for Alison. She did not want me at all. She would not lie down on me and refused to take anything from me. She wanted her mummy. Alison was at the door and I told her to leave, it was fine. I would look after her; Alison needed some alone time, even if it was just ten minutes. In the end, Alison was away for nearly half an hour and Lucia screamed for over half of that time. Eventually, though, she tired herself out and then wanted me to cuddle up on the bed. I kicked off my shoes and climbed onto the bed and lay down. Lucia lay on my chest and the Disney marathon started. Alison returned to find Lucia on my chest and close to sleep. She did her best to stay out of Lucia's eyeline, but it didn't work. Lucia lifted her head and saw Alison and then she wanted her. Alison was shattered but climbed onto the bed after I had been evicted, and Lucia cuddled up with her and was asleep within minutes.

While Lucia was asleep we spoke about the night and then the nurse came around and explained that Lucia was not even drinking half of what was required. We compared their notes to ours and they explained how the amount of food is converted to a liquid amount;

our recordings showed slightly more intake than what the nurses had on their file. Alison and I were very tired for different reasons that morning. We spent most of the morning with Lucia, giving her medicine, milk, and ice cream and other treats. Lucia made great progress that morning. She wanted to get out of bed and explore so I took her to the outside play area. It had a giant pirate ship climbing-frame in the middle, and Lucia had lots of fun out there. I decided that I could use the play area to make sure she kept eating and drinking. I had water and milk with me, and every five to ten minutes I would ask her to come and have some. At first she was compliant and came and drank. After a while, though, she started to refuse to have anymore. I could not even tempt her with ice cream or a chocolate muffin. I told her that unless she drank and ate we would have to go in. No eating and drinking meant no playing. She got upset about it. She had some more water, although not as much as before. After five minutes I asked her to have some more, and she did. She realised that for her to get to play, she had to drink and eat. She had as much as she could.

The afternoon and early evening were very much the same. Lucia ate and drank lots of water and milk. In terms of milk, she had nearly had as much as she would do at home, so Alison and I were feeling very positive. Alison was slowly starting to fall asleep, so we made the decision that she would go home that night. She would be able to rest and not have to worry about the other two, as they were at her parents' house. She would be able to sleep and wake up when she chose, without having to worry about making breakfast or anything. She said she would wait for the evening round and update, and then go home. We sat and waited. Lucia slept and watched Disney films. She was happy with either Alison or me in bed, but wanted one of us with her at all times. I climbed in with her and got ready for a few more hours. Alison sat in the chair waiting and resting.

The nurse came in and said that the chart for today was a lot better than yesterday. We were pleased and smiling, thinking that maybe we could be going home tomorrow. But then came the dreaded words you do not want to hear in a hospital: 'Lucia's intake is just above half what she needs and therefore she still needs to drink more.' Our faces dropped and our shoulders dropped a little too. The nurse must have seen this as she walked off saying sorry. We looked at each other and said we would see tomorrow. We were both exhausted and decided to call it a night. Alison told me that every few hours I would need to wake Lucia up to have her medicine. They had reduced it during the day by removing the Calpol. Every four hours the nurses would wake me.

The night was predictable. Every four hours or so I was awoken to give Lucia her medicine and see if she would have some water afterwards. Lucia woke up and had some water, although not enough to reach the daily quota imposed by the hospital. I slept very well on a pull-out bed next to Lucia's bed in the corner. Lucia was very good during the night; she woke up for her medicine and generally took it without much of a fight and had some water afterwards. She then went back to sleep.

Day four, and Lucia was smiling again. It had been a while since her little smile had been there. She had been, and still is now, a very happy, smiley little girl. Despite everything, she is always laughing, smiling and giggling. That morning she had her little smile back. She was happy and shouted out, 'Daddy!' when she woke up. I pretended to be asleep next to her. She then shouted out, 'Daddy!' again. I turned over and told her to go back to sleep: 'It's not morning yet.' She laughed and said that I was a silly daddy as it was light outside, which means it was morning. She said that she wanted ice cream for breakfast and then to go and play on the pirate ship. I said, 'Of course – but we must make sure we drink lots of milk and water.' I said we would go and get a chocolate muffin as well for breakfast with her ice cream. She smiled and clapped and was so excited that she asked for her milk then and there.

Lucia had her milk, followed by some water, and then she had ice cream, and this time she finished the lot. She was eating much better. We went out of the ward and got her chocolate muffin as I had promised, and I said she could eat it at the table near Costa or we could take it to the pirate ship. She asked if she could take it to the pirate ship and eat it while playing. I do not think that I was meant to take Lucia out of the ward; however, we had been at the hospital, and that ward in particular, many times for therapy; Lucia, Alison and I were known to several nurses, specialists and doctors, and I think this was why we were allowed off the ward. We went back into the ward and headed straight to the play space with the pirate ship. Eight a.m., and Lucia had already drunk milk, eaten, and was now playing. Today was going to be a very good day if it continued as it had started.

Alison turned up just after lunch. She had slept until 11 a.m. – nearly thirteen hours of sleep. She was looking refreshed and ready for another day. Lucia was extremely happy to see her and wanted to take her to the pirate ship and show her what she had been doing all morning. I had arranged for painting in bed to be set up for just after lunch, so I thought this would be good. Lucia took her medicine and had more milk and was still drinking nearly as much as at home. And she was eating things such as toast. Not much, but at least she was having a few bites, which was all good for her recovery.

The nurse confirmed that Lucia still needed to drink more, and Alison and I explained briefly that this was not possible as she did not drink that much anyway. The nurses were working on a chart that based the children's intake on their age.. The problem was, although Lucia was nearly three years old, she had the stature of a lot smaller child. Plus, she had never had an appetite. She generally lived on fromage frais yogurts and the odd chip, and prawn crackers from the local Chinese take-away. Alison and I explained all this again, and in the end I told them to explain to the doctor that what they wanted was never going to happen, so they would not be able to discharge us based on fluid intake. The nurses went to speak to the doctor, and we were told that the doctor was at a conference that day but would come and see us afterwards.

At around 8 p.m. we were wondering if the doctor was still coming or not. The nurse explained that he was, but that the conference was in the middle of London and had been scheduled to finish around 6 p.m. Not that many conferences finish on time; I can speak from experience: most of the conferences I have attended over-ran. Plus, there would be lots of colleagues mingling after the event who may not have seen each other for a while. We got ourselves some dinner and sat down with Lucia ready for another Disney film for the evening.

I think I was in the chair reading my Kindle when, just gone 9 p.m., the doctor arrived on the ward. He went and got Lucia's intake chart and sat with her. He spoke to her about how she was feeling and things. Lucia said that she was okay, but her throat hurt. She wanted to go home. The doctor asked us about her intake and Alison explained about how much milk Lucia had drunk. The doctor compared the nurses' records with ours and found that we had kept accurate records over the whole four days. He was confident that if she drank the same amount during the night and in the morning, he would be able to authorise her discharge. That was the news that we were waiting for. I went home, and Alison said she would call me after the morning rounds, when the doctor had given his decision.

The morning arrived, and after his rounds the doctor did authorise Lucia to go home. He was happy, and Lucia was sitting up, more playful and back to her cheery self. Alison called to say that I would be coming up to collect them instead of visiting. I called Alison's parents and said that I would pick up the girls on my way to the hospital as we were picking Lucia up. I agreed that we would drop by on the way home, too, so they could see her, as they have not been able to come up to the hospital. I collected some things and cleared up the house ready for when they came home. I left the house around 9-ish and collected the girls. They were super-excited about going to see Lucia, and even more so when I told them that we were bringing her home with us. Anabella was so excited that she was jumping up and down and was quite uncontrollable.

We arrived at the hospital and went straight to the ward. Lucia was sitting on the bed painting, one of her treats for drinking plenty. I saw that she had two empty ice cream cartoons there, so she had clearly regained some kind of appetite. Lucia was equally excited to see her sisters. She climbed off the bed and ran to them and gave them both big cuddles and then told them to follow her. The girls did not need to be told twice, and followed her through the ward. Lucia was heading to the pirate ship. Lucia was running as best as she could, which was really more like a speed walker than a runner.

They all arrived in the empty playroom and Lucia pushed the big double doors at the back of the room, which opened out onto the outside play area containing the pirate ship. Anabella and Sofia were surprised how big the ship was and the amount that they could do on it. I settled down on one of the many wooden benches around the outside, and the girls ran to the pirate ship and climbed over and under and through it. Alison came and told us that we would be able to leave after lunch. We stayed out and played, making sure that Lucia kept coming to have water every fifteen minutes. She also had her milk every hour now. Alison and I agreed that we would have lunch at the hospital and then go straight to her parents'.

The doctor came and saw us and explained that we needed to keep doing what we were doing: water, little and often, to keep the wound clean. Any food or milk had to be followed by water. Keep the Nurofen up for at least another week to ten days, to help with the swelling. After that, if she complained of pain then give her Nurofen; if she is in lots of pain then bring her back in, as could be an infection. He also explained that in about three months Anne would be in contact to start speech therapy to see if the operation has been successful or not. We looked at each other after hearing this, knowing that we could have gone through all this for nothing. The whole experience was nerve-wracking, although not as bad as the heart. For one thing, it was not as serious, for obvious reasons. However, Lucia had a compromised immune system, so it was still dangerous when she was put under general anaesthetic. Secondly, the area of the operation was not a major organ. Worst case was that she would not talk. And as she hardly ever talked up to that point anyway, it would not be that big a difference. Thirdly, once you have been through a major operation in which there was a high risk of death, both during the operation as well as post-operation, over which you had no control, you seem to get a different perspective of things. I know that my attitude and viewpoint on things had changed dramatically since Lucia's heart operation.

We got our discharge papers and packed up the car ready to go home via the grandparents. I drove straight there, and they were both excited to see Lucia. Alison's sister was also there to see Lucia. Lucia loved being the centre of attention. What she did not know (and neither did we) was that she would have to go through all this a few more times. We stayed there for most of the afternoon until we all got tired, and then we went home together.

Post operation – what happened next?

In short, nothing at all. The operation made no difference to Lucia's speech at all. Anne started her therapy after three months, and within two months she explained that the same sounds were being made and that her opinion was that nothing had changed. They would need to do some tests and check, but would not be able to do that until the wound had completely healed, which would be another three to four months.

The operation was deemed unsuccessful from the perspective of her speech. However, in terms of her appetite it was a massive success. She started to eat, and try food that she would not try before. She would try chicken nuggets from McDonald's. (She did not like them, but she tried them.) We would go out for dinner and she would try all sorts of things. After several attempts and lots of full plates going back to the kitchen, she finally finished her plate. It was TGI Fridays' chicken strip meal. This was three pieces of breaded chicken and chips. Lucia liked it, and it was the only food that she would finish. As a result, any time we went out to eat as a family it was at TGI Fridays. Now we know the manager and all the staff at the branch we go to; and at ten years old, Lucia tries a lot of things – I would say she is like any other ten-year-old with food. Fussy to some extent, yes – certain things she will like and others she will not even try.

Although the palate operation was not a success in itself, Alison and I believe it was a huge success for Lucia's development. The school were very good with Lucia in ensuring that she was drinking enough water. Lucia tried to fool the staff. I have no doubt that she was in pain and it did hurt, but she knew which members of staff would let her get away with not drinking and which would not. We were very firm with the school that Lucia needed to have water on her desk during the day and that the staff needed to make sure that she drank – force her if need be. She could do it, we knew, as she drank at home and we did not have many battles at all. The only battles over water would be towards the end of the day where she was tired.

In the end, Lucia was assigned a specific member of staff, who was excellent for her. She was just like us as parents. She did not let Lucia get away with any of that playing-up. I understand that it is not good to have your child crying and being in pain. It is very difficult, but Alison and I both believed we knew our daughter well enough to know when she was genuinely poorly. Her behaviour changes, her attitude and her demeanour declines, and you can see the change a mile away. This is probably one of the hardest parts of being a parent: understanding your child and knowing them as an individual. Then making the decisions that are best for them and not for you.

Operation Two:
After the roof of her mouth had healed and further x-ray tests had been taken, it was confirmed that the first operation had done nothing to help her soft palate reach the hard palate at the top of her

mouth to control the flow of air. Nearly twelve months later and we were back in the same large therapy room in the hospital with Anne and the doctor. He had brought some other doctors as well to discuss the best course of action for Lucia. After watching the latest black and white x-ray video of Lucia speaking into the microphone, it was decided that the best option was to add a bump to the back of her throat. He described it like a speed bump you get on the road. It would reduce the gap. There are difficulties with this kind of procedure, hence the additional doctors. The key one was that as Lucia was still growing, her mouth was still developing and so the man-made bump could close the gap and stop her breathing through her nose. The difficulty therefore was agreeing how big or small the bump should be. Because the bump would come from skin and muscle within her mouth, they did not have unlimited resources to use. And there could be lots of issues later if they had to do multiple operations in the same place, so they would have to try and make sure that the operation was done only once, and correctly.

The last issue was that one of the doctors believed Lucia's tonsils were too big to perform the operation successfully for the size of bump that they required. After a lengthy discussion between the doctors, they decided that they would have to remove her tonsils. The speed bump operation was postponed for at least nine months to allow the tonsils to heal properly.

Lucia was booked in to have her tonsils removed a month later and this was done successfully. Lucia was extremely tearful afterwards, just as she was before. A few days of eating ice cream and she was fine. The hospital was focused on consistent water intake to keep the wound clean. Lots of Nurofen was needed to help with the swelling. Upon discharge we were informed that Anne would arrange for therapy to start after nine months to test if the mouth has healed properly before restarting the tests for the speed bump operation.

Lucia was in year one at Willowbrook Primary School at this point. She was doing well in school. She was still signing more than talking, and using picture cards to explain things, especially when she was getting too hot or poorly. The school were getting used to her limited speech, which meant that Lucia was not getting as frustrated as before and reacting. Lucia would communicate orally at home more than sign, unless she was really tired or not feeling great, in which case she would not even try and talk, but just sign for milk or water or a biscuit. As the school staff got more used to Lucia's speech, she became a lot more confident in talking. The latest operation, sadly, reduced her confidence as it was sore, and therefore she relapsed back into her old habits of signing and using picture cards without trying to speak. We worked with the school and told them to make her talk. We understood that this would take longer to explain something, but it was important for her development as well as her recovery. The school agreed.

Lucia did not like being forced to talk, as you can imagine, but it was only short term, and as a result her confidence came back and continued to grow. She was given main roles in school plays. She was signing along with the others, and a lot of children looked to Lucia when they were signing, while Lucia in turn kept trying to speak as much as possible. She read books out loud and asked Anabella to help her. The school said that her friends would also try to help her with pronouncing her words.

Ten months later, they started to the look at the speed bump operation again.

Operation Three:
The same pre-operation tests were conducted. Anne did her checks and confirmed that over the course of nearly a year no improvement had come. Lucia's speech and palate sounds were still the same. She was unable to continue therapy. And so, nearly twelve months later, we were back in the same room with the same doctors.

The latest black and white x-ray video of Lucia speaking was shown on the monitor and it looked like the gap had increased. I was confused and slightly concerned. The doctor explained that the gap looked larger now due to the tonsils being removed. This gave a false impression that the gap had increased.

The doctors asked Lucia to open her mouth and looked inside with their torchlights, and were happy that there was now enough space to do the speed bump operation. They discussed the size again, and said they would know more when they open Lucia's mouth up. They might change the size of the speed bump slightly, depending on what it looked like during the operation, but they had a plan.

As before, the doctor gave us a date there and then, which was in three weeks' time. We said yes and then prepared the school, friends and family and work for the next operation, her third in three years.

Additional schoolwork was prepared, as we planned for at least two weeks off school.

This being the third major operation that we had to prepare for, we now had a system. We knew what the plan was. Alison would take Lucia in, as Lucia always wanted her just before and straight after an operation. My job was to take the girls to school and nursery, and put them in after-school clubs or arrange for friends to collect them if possible.

The operation was scheduled for a Wednesday as before. I had arranged with work that I would be off for the rest of the week. I would then contact them on Friday when I had an update, and discuss the plan for the following week then, or on Monday, if we were still in the hospital over the weekend. Based on previous experience, I was expecting to be in over the weekend and maybe work from home for a couple of days before going back into the office. Alison had prepared the bag and we had woken Lucia up at around 4:30 a.m. to give her milk, as she was not allowed any fluids for two hours before arriving at the hospital. She was due in for 7 a.m. Lucia had her milk and a good amount of water to settle herself. She then went back to sleep until 6 a.m., where she was woken up again.

Alison and Lucia arrived at the hospital just after 7 a.m. and went straight to the ward. The nurses showed her to the bed we were going to have. This time we were in a private room off to the side. Alison dumped all the things in the corner. Everything is the same in the side rooms, the only difference being that instead of the chair that you get in the main ward, you get a pull-out bed. This is slightly more comfortable, although when you are woken up every few hours to give medicine and milk and water it does not make that much difference in my opinion. I would end up so mentally and physically shattered at the end of hospital days with Lucia that I could happily fall asleep on the floor for a few hours.

Lucia's paperwork was all completed, and around 7:30 the nurse told Alison that Lucia should start getting prepared for her operation. This meant the big bath which she could nearly swim in. She was still very small and able to submerge her whole body. Lucia has said that her favourite part of her time in hospital was the massive bath before the operation and the painting in bed afterwards. The nurses told Alison that the surgical team were ready for her now. The porter would be on his way to bring her down. Lucia was dressed in her gown and placed on her bed and there she waited with the iPad for the porter.

He arrived shortly and disconnected her bed from the wall and pulled the safety bars on both sides of the bed up so Lucia was safely inside for the ride down to theatre. She was lying on the bed with a teddy bear that we had purchased on a holiday in the USA because it was wearing the same pyjamas as her. This same teddy bear had been in every operation since her heart, and even now it is the toy she goes to when she feels poorly. The teddy had to be fully washed before every operation as well.

So Lucia and her teddy and Alison were taken downstairs and into the pre-theatre room with the anaesthetist. He was told that Lucia wanted the balloon like before. Lucia sat on Alison's lap, ready to go. Alison placed the balloon over her mouth and nose. Lucia fought a little bit as she was bigger now, but not for very long. She was asleep within ten seconds and then she was picked up and placed on the operation table ready to go in. Alison walked out of another theatre room wondering when she would see her again.

I had dropped Anabella off at school and told the school that I would call after the operation, as Anabella would worry until she knew that the operation had been completed. I told the school to place Anabella in after-school club. Sofia was going to be picked up from nursery by a friend as they did not have a late finish. I would collect her after picking up Anabella. I drove up to the hospital and was directed to Lucia's room by the nurse when I walked onto the ward. Alison was sitting there in the chair reading a magazine.

She explained that Lucia had fought the balloon a little longer this time round, and that made her sad. She was still very nervous and worried about Lucia. We had a few hours to wait before they would be telling us anything. We decided to go out to the main foyer to get a hot chocolate for me and a bottle of Coke for Alison, mainly for a change of scenery and a little walk. Something to distract us while we waited. I have found that waiting for news is more mentally exhausting than anything else.

Lucia was back in the room after nearly four hours. She was very croaky and did not look herself at all. Alison was worried. Lucia stayed asleep for an hour or so and then the nurses came to wake her up. She was not impressed. She woke up crying and screaming and wanting Alison. She refused to take water or milk, and at one point refused to take her medicine. The nurses said that she had to take her medicine or they would have to put the IV line into her. Lucia understood about the IV line, and did not like it, so Alison sat on the bed with her and after ten to fifteen minutes she finally took all her medicine.

An hour later, she was very sick. Amazing, really, considering that there was not much fluid inside her. We cleaned her up and then she went to sleep. For the next four hours, Lucia would wake up from time to time and be a little sick. Some water and fluid would go in, but then she would throw it back up again. This was probably one of the worst first days we had following an operation. She was so pale, and she could hardy stay awake for longer than an hour. She also looked so frail and thin, like she had lost half her weight during surgery. For someone like Lucia who has not much weight or fat at all, looking like she had lost half of it was like staring at a skeleton lying on the bed.

The rest of the first day and night remained that same. Alison explained that there were several screaming fits with Lucia when she was told to have medicine or water. She would eventually take it but was extremely tiring for both Alison and Lucia. Alison did not have much sleep that night.

I arrived the following day and saw that Alison was shattered and so was Lucia. Alison was in the middle of a battle with Lucia over the taking of medicine. I tried to help but Lucia did not want me at all and Alison was getting more and more stressed. I told Alison to just leave and have a break like before. Lucia screamed and cried more and was shouting for her mummy. Alison returned fifteen minutes later, calmer and very determined.

She sat on the bed with Lucia and explained, in her no-nonsense way, that Lucia would not be able to go home until she ate and drank. She knew what she must do, we had done this twice before now. She also said that she would go home if Lucia continued to be silly with the nurses and with medicine. Lucia got very tearful and realised that Alison meant every word. She sat up very carefully and gave Alison a cuddle and said she was sorry.

In the main ward and in the playroom, we had in the past been looked at strangely and even had one parent tell us that Lucia had just had a major operation and that we should give her a break and that we were not helping her. That was her opinion and she was entitled to it; however, I am not sure that same lady would have liked it if I had given my opinion. We seem to be living in a time where people believe that their opinion is fact, and do not like to be challenged. When people feel challenged, then insults are the response. Not a surprise really, when you see world leaders acting in the same way. No names mentioned but I am sure there are a few who spring to mind. Rather than discussing things, trying new approaches and coming to a compromise, they throw insults at each other in Parliament.

The second day was a mixture of sleeping, watching films on the iPad and the start of our drinking games to get Lucia to drink. It worked to some extent. She did not drink anywhere near enough, but it was a start. She was still very tired and not herself at all. The second night Alison stayed as usual. Lucia was not taking many fluids in, the medicine was still a struggle and she was sick once during the night. The bed had to be changed, and Alison took Lucia to the bathroom and gave her a shower. Lucia was extremely tearful. She kept crying and telling Alison that she wanted to come home and she did not want to be in the hospital. It was one of the worst recoveries so far.

Lucia has been in and out of hospitals since she was little. She regards them as part of her normal routine and she looks forward to the hospital in some ways. Mainly it is about seeing the doctors, nurses and therapists she has grown up with. They play games, she tells them how she feels. They do check-ups which they turn into a game with her. She finds out what the next step is, the next operation. She has never once said that she does not want to go to the hospital. Considering how often she has had to go in, Alison and I cannot have her dislike hospitals or have a fear of going.

On the third day Alison gave me an update on the night before. We decided to try and make things as much fun as possible. We got her painting things ready for her in bed. We told her to drink water and milk and she fought a little but as soon as we said that we would stop the painting, she tried more. I took Lucia to the play area outside. She was not very playful and quite slow walking around, but she had a good twenty minutes starting to play. She wanted me to carry her back to bed, so I agreed as long as she drank her water and had her medicine when we get back without a fight. She agreed.

Alison was asleep in the chair when Lucia and I got back. Lucia sat on her bed and put a film on the iPad and I got her water and medicine ready and put it on the table next to the iPad. Lucia leaned forward and took her medicine by herself without any issues, and then drank her water. She was a little tearful afterwards and wanted a cuddle, so I climbed up and we cuddled together watching the film. I fell asleep with Lucia asleep on my chest.

I woke up to the sound of Lucia crying and coughing and then we were both soaking wet. She had been sick all over herself, the bed and me. I got up and started to deal with her. Alison woke up as well. She got towels and things. Went to the ward bathroom and started running the shower and I carried Lucia there a minute or so later. We cleaned Lucia up, put her in her pyjamas; luckily her special hospital teddy did not get wet. I had a quick shower as well and Alison brought me some spare clothes. We had got into the habit of having spare clothes just in case she was sick. We also did not plan ahead which nights we were staying: it depended on how Lucia was that day and how we were feeling as well.

When we got back the nurses had already stripped the bed and were just finishing off tucking the new covers under the mattress. I placed Lucia back into bed and she went straight to sleep. I am sure she fell asleep in my arms before I even put her down.

That evening, Alison went home as she was still very tired. I stayed the third night. I unfolded the visitor's bed, got my pillows all sorted, and then sat in bed reading my Kindle while Lucia was still up waiting for her final medicine for the night, which was due in half an hour. Lucia was watching the same Disney film that we watched earlier. The nurse came around with her medicine and Lucia took it very well, followed by her water. After being sick in the afternoon, she was feeling better.

I settled down for the night and went to sleep. Lucia woke up early on the fourth day. She was already up by the time I woke up. She had paints on her table. She had her water and milk already there. There was also an empty plate covered in crumbs, and two empty yoghurt pots. She said good morning to me and started laughing and smiling. She was clearly feeling a lot better. I asked Lucia what she had for breakfast and wrote it all down in our food and drink diary. She wanted to go and play. She had her water and milk and then jumped off the bed. She had a little more colour back in her cheeks as well. I said I would treat her to a chocolate muffin after playtime if she continued to drink her water and milk. She smiled and took a long swig of her water, as if to prove a point. It made me smile.

The morning was very good. Lucia played in the outside play area, running around and laughing, and we had a good hour of playtime. She drank all her water and I had to get her a refill. She was ahead of her water quota for the morning. She was doing well with her milk as well. We left the ward and went to the main shops in the walkway of the hospital. She got some sweets and a chocolate muffin. We both got hot chocolates as well from Costa. We relaxed, eating and drinking. Lucia was smiling and happy, asking when Mummy was coming and if she could see her sisters. I told her, 'Mummy is coming up later so let's show her how good you have been.' Lucia said okay, and that she was hungry. She asked for more toast with chocolate spread, so we went back to the ward.

I made her more toast, and when I got back to the room Alison was sitting in the chair playing Pairs with Lucia. Lucia was winning, as usual, and drinking all her water. The medicine had been taken as well; the empty syringes were on the table. I put the toast down and Lucia grabbed a slice and started eating. She was biting out big chunks and drinking her water. In the afternoon, Lucia did not drink much milk. She focused on her food. Lots of little things, such as yoghurts; half a slice of toast; half a chocolate muffin or a yum-yum.

In the late afternoon, Alison and I asked if we could go home yet. Lucia was fine, and we believed that she had had enough food and water. The nurses said that she had not. We re-checked our records and checked how Lucia was feeling. She was fine, she was watching a film and drinking more water. Alison asked to see the doctor when the evening rounds were due. Just before the evening rounds were due to start, Lucia got a visitor from her primary school assistant, who has looked after her since she started at the school. She brought her a present and Lucia was so happy to see her. This assistant had been amazing for her. Also, she did not let Lucia get away with missing any therapy or not drinking during the school day after operations.

Lucia is about to go into year 6 in September 2018, and when she leaves, I do believe that her assistant will be in tears, along with Lucia. Year six is a very emotional time for all concerned, the children, the staff and parents. The class has had a lot of characters and a lot of different things that the children have had to deal with, so I think

July 2019 is going to be extremely special.

The doctor came to see us after his rounds were completed. We showed him our records and said we had no concerns over Lucia's food or fluid intake. He went and checked the nurses' records. He re-calculated the food into liquid, and said it was a lot more that the nurses had calculated. Lucia could go home tomorrow. We were happy, and Lucia was even happier. Alison decided to stay that night. I would come and collect them tomorrow, along with her sisters.

The following morning, I came up with Anabella and Sofia. When we got to the room, Lucia was putting on her own clothes, home clothes as opposed to pyjamas. She always loved that part. She knew she was going home. She jumped off the bed and all the girls had a big hug – another thing that always happens when I bring them up to the hospital. The girls all went off to play in the playground outside while Alison and I packed the bags and I took them to the car. When I got back, Alison told me that her parents were coming up and we would all have a late lunch at the hospital while they sorted out the discharge papers.

Alison's parents turned up. We left the ward and went to one of the restaurants. We ordered our food, and all sat down and enjoyed our lunch. We laughed and talked and spoke about all the normal family things: Lucia catching up on her school work, and did Lucia think she would go to school in the next few days or would she be at home for a while? Lucia always wanted to go back to school as early as possible, mainly to see her friends.

The grandparents left after lunch and we went back to the ward to find the discharge papers all done and our copies on the bed. We said goodbye to everyone, including a nurse who we know from our local church, who worked on that same ward. Lucia was happy to be coming home again. Third operation over. We knew we should see progress in her therapy in the next couple of months, and that Lucia should now be able to speak clearly. We were not sure we could handle any more operations after how her recovery went in the first two days.

The post-operation therapy was very good. Anne made good progress with Lucia and she learnt new sounds which she was unable to do before. The speed bump at the back of her throat has managed to close the gap. However, there was still a big enough gap to allow the air to flow. After a few months, Anne advised that she had made progress; however, she thought Lucia needed another surgery as there was still airflow coming through her nose when making certain sounds. There was nothing, therapy-wise, she could do to make any further progress.

So we were heading into operation number four. However, we had two major issues that took place before operation number four could happen.

The first issue was that the doctor who has been looking after Lucia and her palate issues went off on long-term sickness leave and was not available for over a year. Therefore we had a different doctor take over her case. The other issue, which was trickier and something that Alison and I were not prepared for, was this: just after Lucia's latest operation, she had a check-up with her back specialist. He was not comfortable with her back and decided that they were going to put a plaster cast around her torso. I have explained how the cast caused difficulties for Lucia in terms of sleeping and at school, where she missed out on activities such as swimming and had to be very careful playing with other children. During this time, I would say that this was the lowest Lucia had been. The main reason, I believe, is that it was the first time she was unable to do things. Mainly for other people's safety, too, and not for her own. Even after operations, she would still be able to play and do everything else with the other children or with us as a family.

Operation Four:
Operation four took place nearly two years later. One reason was the cast, as they would not do an operation while Lucia was in the cast as they would be unable to get to the vital organs quickly, if need be. The other reason was that there was one less doctor around, so there was a delay. Due to her cast, we were not worried at first. The following summer, once her removable brace was made and she was wearing it, we were in a position to talk about the next operation.

Lucia got used to wearing her brace eventually. She continued her therapy for a short while and then we started to find out what the next steps would be. In the absence of her doctor, Alison and I started the process of trying to find out who was taking over her case. This took a lot longer than it should have done. We had to make numerous phone calls trying to get hold of someone. The therapist kept chasing on our behalf as well. Eventually we managed to get assigned to the doctor who would be taking over.

Sadly, for various reasons, the new doctor and I did not get along. When we were having check-ups and when they did the tests on Lucia to see how her mouth was working and what he thought would be the best option for her, you could feel the tension in the air. It did not make things very productive. I am a very up-front person; I say what I think, probably more than I should. I am also quite direct and literal. I am not someone who says what people want to hear. But the situation was managed, of course, as it was about Lucia, not about me or the doctor.

The new doctor looked at Lucia eighteen months after her last operation. The same pre-operation tests were conducted, and the x-ray video showed the soft palate muscle moving up and down, but not far enough to completely block the airflow. (It is amazing, now, to see the progress Lucia has made after the operations and the speech therapy. As well as her progress with her speech, it has also increased her confidence. She is understood more by others. The school as well as us have learnt what Lucia means when she speaks. We were probably immune to the odd sounds or mispronunciations from Lucia, as we knew what she wanted. However, when she started going to clubs and other events with others who did not know about her speech issues, we were told that she was confident and was understood well by everyone.)

The doctor explained what he thought would be the best thing for Lucia. The operation would tighten her palate muscles by taking some of the skin from her cheeks. This would be the final operation she could have, as there was limited skin remaining on the inside of her cheeks. He also explained that he felt that this was a riskier operation than the others, and therefore he would perform it at Great Ormond Street Hospital (GOSH). We challenged this initially, as this operation seemed to be the same as the previous one in terms of what he would be doing. We did not see how this one was any different. He explained that although it was more or less the same as the previous one, the actual operation was harder and the surgery would take longer because they had operated before. Recovery was expected to be worse for her, and add her DiGeorge condition into the mix and he would prefer to be at GOSH, near the specialist DiGeorge clinic. Lucia was assigned to this clinic, and a lot of her blood tests were reviewed by its team. Also, they provided their opinion on vaccines, such as the MMR vaccine. The DiGeorge clinic did not allow Lucia to have her MMR vaccine as it is a live vaccine which could be dangerous for her.

GOSH was not easy for either of us to get to, as I worked in Canary Wharf and we live in Brentwood in Essex; we would have preferred the Broomfield Hospital in Chelmsford. However, it was not about us as parents. It was about what was the best for Lucia. If GOSH was the safest place for her, that was where her surgery would take place.

The operation was agreed upon. However, because of her brace and a follow-up appointment due shortly, it was agreed that the date would be discussed after that appointment. We had been instructed that Lucia would more than likely wear the brace during the spring to autumn period, and the plaster cast during the winter. So this was the reason for the latest delay: we were expecting her plaster cast to go back on in a few months and that she would wear it until February or March of the following year.

We had the back-specialist appointment, and he was very happy with her. He asked how often the brace was being worn. We told him that Lucia wore it for the majority of the day, and that she had thirty minutes without it for her physio sessions. It came off for her swimming lesson once a week, and we sometimes took it off for a whole day, when her skin was red and needed a breathing day. He was very happy and slightly surprised. He explained that normally the brace was normally removed a lot, as children play up with their parents. We both laughed, as Lucia did try things on. When she was tearful and wanted it off, we had to stand strong together and not give in. And it had paid off, as her back specialist explained that her back was not getting worse. He would not put Lucia in the plaster cast for the winter.

This was amazing news and Lucia was so happy. After being told that she did not need the cast during the coming winter, we contacted the palate doctor and explained that she would not be wearing it, and that the back doctor had no concerns over the surgery. The palate doctor then explained that upon reviewing her records he had requested a heart check-up, as it has been a few years since her last one. He wanted to make sure that her heart could cope with the surgery. Alison and I found this a little strange, but we waited for the heart appointment to be arranged.

The appointment was arranged for after the Christmas period, and in mid-January we went to see her heart doctor, who kept advising us that he was retiring, but then came back as he said he did not enjoy retirement as he was bored. Lucia loves all her doctors and specialists, which makes all these appointments so much easier, especially as we must travel to different hospitals to look at different areas of her care.

Her heart check-up was done. The doctor had no issues, and set her up with another one in five years' time. The results were sent back to the palate doctor and he was satisfied that Lucia was fit to have the operation. He sent us a letter confirming that the operation would take place at Great Ormond Street and was scheduled for a couple of months' time, at the end of May.

Based on previous operations, we suspected that Lucia would be in the hospital for around five days and then have a few days at home before going back to school. I normally work from home on those first few days, just in case I have to collect her from school.

So the operation date arrives. You would think that after so many operations we would be okay, but there are still a few nerves – not as many as with, the heart operation or the other palate operations but there are still some nerves. Not sure if the nerves were a result of the check-ups that took place beforehand: the heart one was worrying for obvious reasons: if her heart had a problem than she could die. And even though the heart check-up was fine, it was still something extra that we had to think about this time round.

This time Alison and I both drove Lucia to the hospital. Anabella and Sofia were staying at a friend's house that morning; I was going to drive the car back and collect the girls later that day. The girls were not at school as it was the holidays. We got to the hospital and we were shown to her ward and her bed. We got all her clothes, toys, iPad, etc. all set up, and then we played games and waited to be told when Lucia was going down. This happened about an hour later.

We all went down and both of us were allowed into the anaesthetist's room to put Lucia to sleep. Lucia has already selected the balloon which would go over her nose and mouth when they turned on the gas. Alison held Lucia on her lap and placed the balloon over her nose. Lucia fought, and now that she was bigger and stronger she was able to push the balloon off several times. Alison managed to hold Lucia but not the balloon at the same time. I grabbed the balloon and held it over her nose and mouth. Alison held Lucia tight. This battle continued for another minute or so. Eventually Lucia has cried herself tired, and with me holding the balloon while Alison held her arm she had to breathe in deep lungsful of the sleeping gas. She started to fall asleep; she got very heavy and I helped lift her onto the bed ready for her operation, which would take place through the big double doors directly in front of us.

Lucia went through, and we left. We went and got some breakfast. We never had an early breakfast on the mornings of operations, as Lucia was not allowed to eat or drink for hours beforehand and it was unfair to eat in front of her. We left the hospital and walked around Holborn and I found myself a Costa for a hot chocolate. Alison had a toasted tea cake and then looked for a Starbucks for coffee. We both had books or the Kindle to read. We grabbed our drinks after breakfast and went to the nearby park and sat on the bench in the sunshine and read.

The operation took about four hours. We were called to say that she was about to leave surgery and be put in post-op care before transferring to the ward. We were instructed to go and see Lucia there. Normally they only allow one person in, but today Lucia was the only person in post-op care so we were both allowed in. Lucia was screaming loudly. This was unusual. Normally Lucia stayed asleep after an operation, but here they woke her up. This was the doctor's decision. He wanted to see her awake before sending her back to the ward. He was happy, and had already left by the time we arrived. The nurse said that basically she would be there for fifteen to twenty minutes to check that Lucia didn't react after the operation. We sat with Lucia and tried to calm her down. Tried to get her to drink some water or play a game. It didn't work. Alison climbed onto the bed with her and just gave her a cuddle, which seemed to settle her a little; she was still crying, but not as much as she had been before. She also had an NG tube attached to her. She had not had this for a long time, and we realised her throat would be very sore. After previous operations, we were instructed to get Lucia to eat rough food such as toast, to brush against the palate, which helps it to heal. This time, the doctor did not want anything (including water) touching the palate.

The nurse advised that the porter would be coming to collect her and that we could then go back to the ward. It was all done – the final operation. We would not know if it was successful for at least six months when the palate had healed and therapy could start. Up in the ward, the chair that turned into a bed was in the corner. Lucia settled herself and went to sleep. We used the time to grab a drink and some food for ourselves. We would normally get chocolate muffins or yum-yums and other things that Lucia likes, but as she was going to be fed through the NG tube we did not get anything for her yet. There was also a morphine drip through an IV which we had thought was not coming onto the ward. However, we were wrong. The morphine was in the ward as well.

Lucia woke up a few times crying and screaming. She was saying that her throat was sore. She refused to eat or drink anything. Lucia's medicine was given through the NG tube. Alison and I also administered her special milk and water through the NG tube as well.

Alison stayed the first night, and it was a long night. Lucia woke up a lot crying. The morphine was increased once during the night and then was lowered back down again in the morning. Alison did not get much sleep, and in the end fell asleep on Lucia's bed with Lucia asleep across her chest.

I drove up the next day with both the girls to see if that would help Lucia. Seeing her sisters is always something that gets her excited, and we thought maybe it would help her on her second day in the hospital. I arrived with both the girls. Anabella was extremely excited and slightly hyper, which resulted in her jumping around a little crazy and ending up upsetting Lucia. Sofia was trying to calm Anabella down but wanted to give her other sister a kiss and cuddle and was conflicted. In the end, Anabella went off to find the playroom and Sofia climbed onto the bed and gave Lucia a cuddle and tried to read her a book.

Sadly, having her sisters with her did not improve Lucia's mood. She remained in bed and not happy. There was still lots of crying and saying that she was in pain. I took the two girls to the playroom for a bit and then went to go and get lunch. There is a Byron burger restaurant near Holborn tube station and this became her favourite choice for food. Take-away Byron burgers. I got back with the girls after lunch to see Lucia being cleaned up. Her bed was covered in milk and the NG tube had been removed. Lucia had been sick, and all the milk had come up. While she was being sick she had pulled the NG tube out. The nurses along with myself cleaned Lucia's bed while Alison took Lucia to the bathroom to give her a shower.

When Lucia was clean and dry, she got back into bed and put a Disney film on the iPad and watched it and fell asleep. Now with no NG tube, she would have to be woken to take her medicine orally, along with milk and water. Although she was sick, she still needed to eat and drink before she could come home. The other big issue was her temperature. It kept rising and falling. It was all over the place. GOSH had temperature strips which must be held under the armpits. Not easy when Lucia was not wanting to be touched or just wanted to sleep.

The rest of the second day was mainly focused around managing her temperature and trying to get her to drink water. The milk was not touched, but Lucia started taking little sips of water, usually only after being given medicine every two hours. I took the girls home after we had got Lucia settled. Alison explained to Lucia that she needed to eat because the NG tube was not being put back in, or she was not coming home. Lucia was not happy about that. She wanted to come home. She kept saying that she wanted to go to sleep in her own bed. Alison got her some ice cream and a yum-yum, along with some painting to do in bed. Lucia sat up, not feeling very well and not very happy about it. She had a bite of the yum-yum and cried, as it was painful. She had some water and said that this felt extremely sore as well. She did not manage to do anything for more than five minutes, but it was better than before. The night was a lot better for Alison.

On the third day, I dropped the girls off at a friend's house and drove up to see Lucia and Alison. Alison said that she had had a better night. Lucia was sitting up slightly. Still no smile, though. No smile for two days. She tried to talk some more. She was asking for water as opposed to pointing. We gave her treats as usual. This time we reduced the amount that she needed to do to get a treat. We played drinking games with games of Pairs and Snap. I brought the painting things to her bed. The morning was very slow and quiet. The afternoon started to slowly improve. Lucia wanted to sit up higher and wanted to paint again. She grabbed the yum-yum from the plate by her bed and ate a little more. She took a small bit and then put it down. We set up a reward chart to get stars when she drank, ate or had her medicine. The late afternoon was better, with Lucia seeming more herself. She was smiling a little.

Alison decided that she would go home that night and I would stay. Lucia may have influenced Alison's decision. I got my things ready for the evening, Alison packed up hers and went out to get us dinner, a take-away from Byron (again). Lucia and I read stories on the bed while waiting for dinner. I tried to convince Lucia to read some words with me. She did not want to at first. After a few pages, though, she wanted to read. She read very slowly, and it was great. I got her water and she drank as she read.

Alison arrived with the burgers and chips. I sat on the end of the bed and Lucia said she was going to continue reading. Alison and I ate our dinner and were smiling, feeling proud of our little angel. Lucia got very tired after her reading and fell asleep before we finished our dinner. Alison went home and planned be back up just after lunch. I put the pull-out bed together and got ready for bed. Lucia stayed asleep all night.

The morning of day four. Lucia woke up early and wanted ice cream and toast. This was a good sign. She managed to eat a quarter of the toast. I enjoyed the rest and Lucia had a few teaspoons of ice cream. She kept the ice cream, and over the course of the next hour she took a teaspoon every ten minutes. I got her paints and pictures to paint in bed. We also got her new reward chart for the day and agreed to see if we could get ten stars for food and drink each. Lucia was smiling and excited about getting it. She asked for a present when she got out of hospital. I asked her what she wanted. She asked for a Woody doll from Toy Story, one of the Disney films that seemed to be on repeat on the iPad. I said that if she kept going today and took her medicine and had her milk, water and food without complaining and had more than yesterday, then I would get her the doll.

We played Pairs and other card games, which resulted in her having sips of water and milk when she got a pair. I would not aim to win the game, I would aim to make sure that she was always just ahead so she did not feel like I was not trying. After a few games, though, I was not even trying to let her win; she had become too good. Even when I tried to win, I lost. Lost badly as well.

The morning went very well. She continued to paint and eat. I teased her with a chocolate muffin and she was super-excited. She drank more milk and water, and according to our notes she was just below the recommended amount set by the doctor. Lucia asked to go to the playroom. We both went and played. We played lots of different games and Lucia kept drinking. We played for over an hour; it was the most she had played since the operation.

We returned to find Alison, Anabella and Sofia in the ward waiting for Lucia. Lucia ran straight towards her sisters and gave them a big cuddle and kisses. She jumped up on Alison's lap afterwards and did the same to her. She showed Alison her chart, trying so hard to speak, but it was still very sore. She was unable to speak for very long and so resorted to pointing to the charts. She was eating and drinking.

The rest of the afternoon was not as good. Lucia got very tired – too much excitement in the morning, I suspect. She sat on her bed, wrapped up, with Anabella next to her in bed. They cuddled each other, and Sofia sat on the edge of the bed with her feet on the back of the chair watching the iPad. Have a guess which Disney film. Yeah, you guessed it. Toy Story (again).

Alison and I relaxed, and I thought that I would be taking the girls home. I started packing my things up. Lucia noticed. She didn't want me to go, she wanted me to stay that night again. Alison was happy to go back that night and would stay the following night. So we all tried to group together watching the rest of Toy Story. It is very difficult for five people to cuddle up, plus, the table over a hospital bed is very small. Watching anything on an iPad is difficult unless you are directly in front of it. Alison and I were not directly in front and obviously were never going to win a battle against three girls and a Disney film. Alison had a surprise for Lucia. She had brought up noodles from our local Chinese restaurant.

Lucia loved those noodles. She ate lots of them, nearly the whole box, which was not a small amount, as the owner knew us. The girls enjoyed some Chinese dinner as well, which was heated up in the parents' kitchen. It was really nice having a family dinner together with one of our favourites. It is generally very difficult for us as a family to agree what food we eat. We each want something different, so Alison ends up making multiple meals for us. Sometimes I think she is running a restaurant. Alison took Anabella and Sofia home and I settled in for another night with Lucia.

This time, she was awake in the night. She was hungry and thirsty. We sat up in bed watching more Disney films, although I refused to watch Toy Story again. I was all Toy Story'd out by this point. So Lucia found another Disney film to watch and I settled in for cuddles and the film. We had drinks and I got some sweets as well, and we pretended to be hiding from the nurses and doctors, who would say that it was late and that we should be sleeping and should not be eating chocolate and sweets. When the nurses came in, we would hide our sweets. The nurses laughed. They would join in and check that we were asleep. We would pretend to be asleep. Lucia was not very good at this game; she laughed under the covers when the nurses came and checked the bed. (She has got better at it now, as when I come and check on her at bedtime she is very quiet and doesn't laugh. She hides books in her bed, and, when I go downstairs at bedtime, turns on a torch and reads like Harry Potter does in one of the films.)

Day five. This was a very uneventful day really. Lucia was playful. She was eating and drinking well. Alison brought Anabella and Sofia up again. They all went off to the playroom. Lucia was still drinking and eating. They watched Toy Story 3 and Lucia asked for a Jessie doll as well as a Woody doll. She kept asking. She asked when the doctor came around and was checking the chart. We asked if we could go home. He said he would be happy for that to happen if Lucia did well this afternoon. The day before she had dipped a little, but if she hit the target today, he would agree at evening rounds. At that point I promised Lucia that she could have a Woody and a Jessie doll. She was really excited, grabbed the milk from the table and had a big drink from it.

The girls had a great afternoon together. I joined them in the playroom and played lots of different games. Lots of colouring and so on. (I have a special colouring book, pencils and pens which I use to calm down and when I am stressed. I find that colouring helps me process things when too much is going around me. The girls love colouring, too.) Later that afternoon the doctor came around and checked the charts and was happy. However, he wanted to keep Lucia in overnight. Alison stayed that night and I agreed to take the other two home and collect Alison and Lucia in the morning. We would go straight to the shops to see if we could get her the Woody and Jessie dolls.

Alison had a good night; she sat on the bed watching Toy Story again, as Lucia was excited about getting her dolls when she gets out of the hospital. The final night was generally the quietest of all, as everyone knew that we were finally going home the next morning.

The next morning, Alison got all the things packed up and put the bags next to the bed ready for me to collect. Lucia got into clothes that she could go shopping in when we left. She had two whole slices of toast and ice cream. She drank her milk and sat on the bed ready to go home. Alison said that she was extremely jumpy that morning. All excited about the Toy Story dolls.

I drove up, collected the bags and Alison and Lucia, and we came home. I went to pick up Anabella and Sofia from our friend's house before going out that day. The afternoon was really nice. All of us shopping at Smyth's superstore. Lucia found the Woody and Jessie dolls. We got them, and Lucia was so happy. The problem with them was that they were quite big and heavy for her. Lucia struggled to carry them for long. She recovered well, though, and both of those dolls now are in her bed – every night.

Operation Five:

I have said that the fourth operation would be her final one as there is nothing else the doctors can do about Lucia's palate. However, she does now have a minor operation scheduled for October 2018. We were advised that there would be one more, although it is only to remove two 'pockets' from her mouth.

This operation is to remove the pockets that were created in the last operation. The pockets are designed to help the blood flow during in the recovery process. Different doctors have different opinions as to when it is best to remove them. There are three trains of thought when it comes to the removal of these pockets:

Doctors that believe they can be removed shortly after the previous operation;

doctors that believe they should leave them for at least a year before removal; and finally

doctors that believe that unless they are in the way and doing harm they can remain.

The doctor who did the last operation was in the second group. He believed that they should remain for at least a year to help with the healing process and then be removed. However, since the last operation, he has left the hospital and is no longer part of Lucia's care team. Our main doctor was still off at the time when he left, but he is now back. He returned to the hospital in the summer of 2018 and is part of the first group: he believes that they should be removed as soon as possible. As part of returning to work, he reached out to all his patients and got a status update. He has scheduled an appointment with Lucia and scheduled a time for the removal of the pockets.

During our meetings, he said he wanted Lucia in as early as possible; however, Lucia is now in year six of primary school. She has her year six trip away for a week in early September, and we have lots of events planned during the summer holiday period. Her speech therapist was present during these appointments and she advised that Lucia is making excellent progress with her speech, so the removal of the pockets is not a priority.

As Lucia has missed out a lot due to her operations, especially as the majority of her operations have been around her birthday in April, we want to make sure that Lucia enjoys her final year. This is a big year for her. Year six is an important year for children, including socially, so we want to make sure that she did not miss out on any of the planned events. As it is her last year, we want her to experience and enjoy as much of it as possible.

The doctor is fully aware of Lucia's recovery issues, and our understanding is that Lucia will be allocated a bed on a just-in-case basis. We have some pre-operation checks due at the end of September 2018 and then we will have a day surgery operation, fingers crossed.

The only change that we know will happen is that Lucia will no longer have the balloon to put her to sleep. She is now too big and strong to be held and have the balloon over her face. This time she will have an injection instead. Lucia is used to needles, having had many blood tests, and is not bothered by them much. However, the needle for being put to sleep is twice as long as a blood test one and has to be inserted and then taped down, so it is more uncomfortable.

16 – SOFIA

I have tried to explain about the conditions that Anabella and Lucia have. Now I would like to explain how Sofia, the youngest daughter and a child without any additional or complex needs, interacts with her sisters, from the normal sibling rivalry to visiting her sister after hospital operations. I also would like to share some of the things Alison and I did as parents which seemed to work well, and some of the mistakes we made when focusing heavily on one child temporarily, like during a hospital operation.

Sofia acts very differently at home than she does when she is out with her sisters. This is not unusual, as all children behave one way at school and one way at home and with relatives. Sofia is extremely protective of both her big sisters when we are out. Lucia is treated like the youngest sister, as both Anabella and Sofia protect her when we are in public. Sofia comes across as the main protector of the three.

Anabella, especially when she was younger, was very active and had no sense of personal space. She would therefore put herself in situations whereby she would invade others' personal space. Everyone reacts differently to situations like this. Some people would back away from Anabella, while others would ignore her or not seem to mind. Some took exception to having their personal space invaded, especially children. Whether out and about or at school, Sofia would be the one who would try and get in between Anabella and the other person if need be. As I have said, everyone reacts differently. Children react directly, as that is one of the beautiful and equally frustrating things about the young. They say what they think. They also do what they think is correct. As you grow up, you learn acceptable behaviour by observing others and making mistakes and learning from them. Anabella does not learn quite like others due to her autism. Sofia was the one who would understand a situation and try and pull Anabella away to make things more comfortable. She would try to explain the situation to Anabella; at other times she would ensure that any negative reaction against her would end there.

Sofia is extremely protective of both her sisters. I am not sure exactly why she is so protective. She is aware that both her sisters have complex needs and that socially they find certain things difficult. She has seen bullying take place against Anabella and was not very happy about it. One example that I always remember is a trip to the park where there were older children playing. Anabella tried to play with them, but due to her particular social skills ended up upsetting some of them rather than befriending them. As a result, the older children pretended to play with her but ended up taking the micky out of her, mocking her and making her chase them around knowing that she would not be able to catch them. This is one of those things that happens with children growing up. I experienced it myself when I was younger, and it is a situation that children learn to deal with. Most children work it out and then one party stops or goes home and generally that is the end of it. Anabella, however, did not understand what was happening and did not realise that she was being made fun of. Sofia did though. She was not impressed, and after a little while she told Anabella to stop playing with the others and tried to get her to play with her instead. One of the older children, who was maybe eleven years old, kept encouraging Anabella to play with them and then the same thing happened again. Sofia, who was six at the time, went and challenged this eleven-year-old girl and told her to leave her big sister alone. She is quite fearless, and I am one of those parents that believes that the best way to learn things is to try, fail, get up and try again. (There are, of course, different circumstances and situations which require a different approach when parenting and learning.) Sofia has seen the lows of both her sisters, and she will do what she thinks is best to protect them.

So Sofia sometimes acts older than she actually is. This is down to several factors. The first is that she is the youngest child. Being the youngest means she wants to do the same things as her elder sisters. As a family we try and do things that all three can do. As parents, Alison and I try and promote as much independence as possible. There are two reasons for this: one is that we believe it is extremely important that our children are independent and feel that they can accomplish anything they set they mind to. The second reason is that due to the numerous appointments that Lucia has had, and their frequency, we are unable to do everything for her and we need Sofia to help us, along with Anabella.

The flip side is that Alison and I have made mistakes through forgetting how old Sofia actually is. She is seven and therefore she still likes playing with dolls. She loves being creative with Play-Doh and such things. But she also has make-up and plays a lot of older games with her sisters. As a result, I believe that Sofia can be prone to attention-seeking when we are focusing on Anabella or Lucia. It is natural that she wants to feel included. She understands that when your sisters are poorly, our attention is not on her. She sometimes just wants to play a game that is more appropriate for her and get more attention. When she is in this mood, which is happening less often now, we try our best to recognise it. She can be very tearful and appear very needy. When we are taking Lucia to the hospital or Anabella is having one of her bad days, Sofia never complains or misbehaves. She is an amazing little girl and either helps us or reads a book or does something else to allow us the time to focus on the other child.

This is why I believe that when she has moments of bad behaviour it is because she would like some attention. She wants us to remember that she is seven and not twelve and that she, like any young child, needs some attention for herself. There is nothing wrong with that at all. As parents, we have to work hard raising three girls. Two of them have additional and complex needs, but does that mean that the third does not need attention? Of course not, she requires as much attention as her sisters.

In the house Sofia is just like any other child with siblings. She plays with them, pushes boundaries and fights with her sisters when they touch her make-up. Each child is different and at a different stage of development and growth. They want different things from Alison, from their sisters, and from me. When children are younger, like five and two, the differences are not so great. They can play the same games together. However, when their ages are twelve and seven, they do not always want to do the same things together.

It is easy to put all your focus on one child, especially when your other child is playing up. If a child has additional and complex needs and requires a lot of attention, it is even easier to put your focus there. Children are resilient and when they are young they manage to work things out. They seem to know when something is not right. They may not be able to explain it. Anabella knew when Lucia was poorly, and that she was different and required extra attention. She could not understand why, or even help, when she was younger. But she knew. She would read or play with Lucia to calm her down. Very similar to how Sofia can calm Anabella down now when she gets anxious or some sudden change happens which results in a meltdown. Sofia knew that Lucia was poorly and when she visited her in hospital she would climb up onto the bed and sit with her and stroke her head or cuddle up to her. She wouldn't play very much, which is unusual for a three-year-old, especially in the games room of the hospital. She would just sit there with her big sister. Holding her hand and just being that presence there.

Try not to feel guilty about it: your focus will shift from child to child regardless of whether your children have any additional or complex needs. It's the same when your focus is on any big project, like when moving to a new house. You prioritise the most important thing at that time. It may not be the most important thing ever, just the most important thing at that stage. If you are moving to a new house in a week and your car's MOT is due in three weeks, you will focus on the house. That does not make you irresponsible about your car. It's the same with children. Focusing on the one child in hospital does not make you an irresponsible parent when it comes to your other children. A family is a big complex dynamic, and attention will shift. One thing that can be helpful is to try and recognise that you are giving more attention to one child, and be clear about the reason behind it. Depending on the age of your other children, you should try and explain what is going on and why your focus has shifted somewhere else. What can you do after that specific focus has ended? Is it a temporary situation that is pulling your focus? Is it permanent? If permanent, then you need to look at things, as permanent situations will require changes short term as well as long term. In a temporary situation, you may not need any changes at all, or small changes for a short period of time.

We have always explained as much as we thought would make sense to Sofia about Lucia. We believe that she now needs to understand the full picture. When Lucia is not feeling great or having a bad time, and with Anabella now at secondary school, Lucia goes to Sofia for help.

There is no easy guide to parenting, or even a guide at all. Everyone has a different approach to bringing up children. Some parents are very open with their children and some shield them from everything. Personally, I think there are good and bad points in each approach, same as with everything in life. You have to find a balance that works for your family and the dynamics of the situation you find yourself in.

I have been asked more times than I can count about how much information should be disclosed to a child. This is one that I cannot answer for anyone aside from my family. I do believe that hiding things never helps. This does not mean tell them every second thing. Sofia is only seven years old. She knows that Lucia had open heart surgery when she was four and half months, and that she could have died. She knows the words, but not the context. She knows that when she has her hospital operations it could be dangerous, although not as bad as the heart operation. She knows she has to have her medicine when she comes out of an operation. She knows that at the hospital we have to make her drink and eat even though it is painful and sore, and she will cry. She knows that one of us must stay at the hospital overnight, and that we swap if she is there for more than four days.

I have made many mistakes with my children and I am sure over the next ten-odd years I will make more. The key thing for me is that I have learnt what I could do better next time, how better to deal with a situation or not create the situation in the first place. The latter is the one I really need to work hard on. Life is difficult enough and you can only do what you feel is right at the time and try not to re-live it repeatedly. You need to put a situation or an event behind you and move on (easier said than done sometimes, I know).

I have spoken to Sofia about how she feels. I wanted to make sure that her views were included here. I have explained how I see things to her, but I think it is good to get the view of Sofia directly: how a seven-year-old girl sees our family and what she knows about her sisters' disabilities.

Sofia explained that she knows Lucia spends a lot of time in hospitals, both for regular appointments, such as her speech therapy once a week in the mornings, and so she goes to school with me, and also that she has had regular operations whereby Mummy and Lucia stay at the hospital and Daddy looks after her and Anabella at home. She enjoys coming up to the hospital afterwards to see her in bed and to play games with her. Sofia loves to help, and she will read stories to Lucia in her hospital bed. She will pass her drinks and makes sure she drinks them, too. Mainly she just loves giving her sister kisses and cuddles; she knows when Lucia is getting better because she gets stronger cuddles back.

Sofia understands that her sisters are 'special' – her word. She knows that they struggle with different things and that Lucia has physical issues which Anabella does not. She loves being able to help them both. She said that when Anabella gets crazy or has a meltdown, she knows that she can help her by reading her a story or making Anabella read her a story to calm her down. She loves being able to help her big sister by herself, without Mummy and Daddy's help.

She also recognises that sometimes she is the reason why Anabella goes crazy. She knows that Anabella has issues with loud noises and understands that when she, Sofia, plays with her sisters or with friends she can get loud and cause Anabella to react. She tries her best to settle Anabella down when that happens. She tries to understand what her sisters need and help them.

For Lucia it is more physical. Sofia will pick things up for her, and as they share a bedroom she will do certain things when they tidy, so Lucia does not have to bend down very often.

I asked her how it makes her feel when our attention is on either of her sisters during an operation, or if Lucia has a seizure, for example. She looked very sad while we were discussing this. She said that she understood that both Anabella and Lucia have moments because of their conditions when they need attention. She understands that she does not figure in moments like that and that she is all alone. Sofia was very sad about this. Saying that she was all alone, she got quite upset. She did say that normally afterwards she gets special attention just for her, like a reward for being a big girl – she loves having both Mummy and Daddy's focus on just her; but she cannot help being sad when she gets no attention.

This was very hard to listen to. I could see that she understood the reasons why she sometimes felt all alone, but it is never easy to hear that from your child.

We had a massive cuddle and Sofia sat on my lap and was interested in this chapter, as she knew that what we were discussing was for this part of the book. After a little cry, she smiled, that big infectious smile, and said, 'What else shall we talk about?' I think this attitude sums both her and the other two up. They know what needs to happen, and that is not easy, and sometimes they feel excluded or ignored, but they also know that it is never on purpose, and only temporary.

I asked Sofia how I could help her so she would not be sad when things happened. She looked at me and said that she was not sure I could: if Lucia is poorly, I have to help Lucia first. But she did ask that I maybe give some more time to explaining what is happening. She said that usually I say it once and that is it. I thought about the last time Lucia had an operation, and saw that Sofia was right.

I have come to the conclusion that because Alison and I are so used to the different appointments and operations, we do not think about it enough. We go on autopilot and therefore maybe do not explain things enough to the other girls. I also think that maybe because the girls have seen it all before and gone through, I feel that I do not need to explain it in detail again. The thing I am forgetting is probably the most important thing: Sofia is seven. She is not an adult. She may have seen it all before and been to the hospital multiple times to visit Lucia, but she is still seven. She needs comfort and attention like any other seven-year-old.

This has reinforced my belief that you need to create separate time with all your children. One-on-one time, as well as family time. Each child is different. Each child will grow up to be an individual. I want to be able to have an individual relationship with each of my children as well as a family relationship. Sofia is the child that keeps me grounded – who reminds me to ensure that individual time with my daughters is equally important as our family time together.

17 – FAMILY LIFE

How does our family work? I wish I knew. It works the way it does because as parents we generally believe the same things with regard to parenting. We both have similar interests as well as different interests that we can share with our children separately.

Alison, for example, is very creative. She does cooking and crafting. She makes bottles, notebooks, all sorts of things which the children love doing. It is something I enjoy from a distance, and although I am not a very hands-on craft-person I love watching them all makes things or giving them ideas for things to make. These are activities that can be done individually and as a family.

The girls and I have football season tickets. For me, it is a time to enjoy my football team and a day out with my girls, just me and them. For them, it is more of a day out with me as opposed to watching the football. They do not actually watch the game, they play with the friends they have made there. Occasionally, one of them may want to sit with me to watch the game and take an interest, and the more we have gone, the more their interest in the game is growing.

We have a dog now, too. The girls love taking her for walks and I have started taking just one of the girls at a time with me while walking the dog. It is a time to walk and relax and talk to each other. Some alone time away from everyone else, to talk about school, say, and how they are feeling, and what do they want for their birthday, or anything else they may want to talk about. It may be that they are fighting with their sisters more at the time, so I can use the walks as a time to talk about it.

The key thing I have worked out is that communication is key. It seems pretty obvious that communication is essential, but I have found that, when everything was going on – all the craziness, hospitals, struggling with health professionals and trying to find out what was wrong with either of my daughters – I actually communicated less. I did not speak to Alison about my feelings, what thoughts were going through my mind. I was not asking her how she was feeling either. I could see that she was not doing great, but I never actually asked her. I tried to be strong for both of us, thinking that she needed me to be strong for us both. This was partly true, but she was feeling the same thing. She thought I was struggling. She thought that me not talking about things was my way of avoiding dealing with the issue. In part, I think she was right. I am a person who tends not to worry about things I cannot control. As a result, I can seem very distant and people may think I do not care. This is not true, but Lucia's heart problem and the fact that she could die on the operating table was something that was out of my control. I could cry, scream, get angry, or be the opposite, be very quiet and unemotional – nothing I did or did not do would change the outcome.

I could however, be supportive to Alison and be open with her about how I was feeling. She was scared to open up and I felt that I shouldn't open up. The result was that we dealt with things separately. And we ended up doing that all the time. We didn't open up over our daughters' health, and then sadly we did that with other aspects of our relationship. We were both going through things and we should have supported each other. We did, in our own way, but not together.

The fact is, we are a family. Regardless of what happens in five days, five months or five years. We will be a family. When the children grow up and maybe have their own children, I will still be their dad. We will still be a family. It is important for our children to know that they can open up to us or their sisters over anything, including when they feel down or scared. So we talk to our children about the importance of opening up.

Also, every family dynamic is different. I cannot tell you what is best for you and your family. I can only share my experiences of my own family. What we have done, what worked for us and what did not work. What we have learnt over the last ten years through two children being diagnosed with disabilities and an adult being diagnosed with autism. The multiple hospital operations and complications that we have had to face as a family, as a unit. It is important to have a support network around you, and in fact I believe that you need two networks to be able to handle anything that you end up facing. One network is your family. Either your immediate family, meaning your partner and children, or your extended family, your parents and siblings. The other network is your friends, people outside your family. You get a different support structure there. Both are key in my experience, although sadly I did not realise that until quite late. I ended up in a place which could have been avoided.

The important thing was that my family was there. They gave me the strength and focus to get out of that dark place. Ensured that I was able to look after myself and then look after others.

Throughout this whole book and nearly the last eighteen years, I have had someone with me who also has gone through all of this with me. Alison. She is the one who manages all the hospital appointments for Lucia and Anabella. She also manages all the school activities, making sure that they have everything ready. School runs. Hospital runs. Ensuring that all parties are aware of what is going on. Communicating with the school when Lucia's assistant needs to come to the hospital. Making sure that the school medical bag is stocked properly. All of this happens through her and her alone.

Alison describes our house as a house of madness. She finds it difficult to gauge everyone's reactions. How I react to something one day compared to the next day. How Anabella will react. How she manages when Anabella and I clash. Alison wonders how it all works as well. She is not sure exactly how it works or why it works after all this time; but it does, in its own way.

This family is no different to any other family. We deal with the issues in front of us. It could be a major meltdown from Anabella or myself; another appointment or operation for Lucia; Sofia growing up and us having to remember that she is seven (at the time of writing) and not fourteen. We do it all as a unit. Like any good team, you have to have faith in each player to do the job assigned to them. We have faith as a family that we all work for each other.

18 – CONCLUSION

I have tried to explain a bit about our conditions and have given some examples of how my daughters manage theirs. I have tried to show how, as a family, we try and manage three daughters, and the complex dynamic we have. Hopefully this will show you that anything is possible and that you should never let anything stop you from doing anything.

For those of you who have any of these conditions or any other condition, keep going. It is not easy progressing through this world sometimes. The alternative, though, not trying or locking yourself away, is no alternative. That option just keeps you in the same place with no hope of change. Tomorrow is another day and no matter how bad today seems, you will go to sleep and wake up in the morning, so you have survived.

For those of you who know someone with additional and complex needs: support them. This part is not easy either. Depending on the needs, they may not be able to express how much they need help or may be unable to communicate this in a way that makes sense. They could even mean something completely different to what they seem to say. Give them a little slack. Everyone needs help. However, the best help is the help they can give themselves. I believe that when you have a condition, the best support involves helping you to manage your condition yourself (if you can). In the case of Anabella, I know that she has many social issues, making friends and losing them just as quickly, especially now she is at secondary school. However, I cannot make her friends. I can just keep asking and trying to explain what the other child could be thinking when she makes an 'inappropriate' comment or gesture. If, say, she keeps repeating the same thing over and over just to make conversation. I can explain how others might feel and try and get her to think about her behaviour. It is no good me saying stop doing something if she does not understand why.

Finally, this book is for those of you who have decided to read it simply to understand more about these kinds of conditions. How another person who needs some additional help sometimes feels when that help is not available or is inadequate. How they see the world around them and how they are sometimes treated. And how you could maybe help. Everyone needs help at some point, and some people need more help than others and over a longer period. Does that make us any different?

When people find out that I am autistic, I get a look of shock from whoever I have explained this to. 'I would never have guessed', they say; or 'you don't look autistic', or my personal favourite: 'Are you sure?' A condition that has few or no physical attributes is still something that we should take seriously. I may not 'look' as if I have additional needs at first glance. I have grown up, had my own family, worked for very large international companies, which has helped me adapt, learn and manage my issues in some ways. It does not mean that I don't have issues. I still have anxiety about many things, I still get frustrated beyond reason if something is not done in the right order. There is no logic behind it. I still take a coat out but rarely wear it. I even wrote this book in a set format based on something that I researched and which seemed to make the most sense to me at the time.

I remember as part of my annual performance review when I worked for a bank, there was a form to fill out and it covered three things. What you should start doing, what you should stop doing, and what you should continue. Parenting is very much like that. If something does not work or is not having the impact that you hope, then stop. Try something new and start that process. Anything that is working well, continue – too often you may stop something because you think a lesson has been learnt or that behaviour has improved so there's no need to continue what you were doing. This is not always the case; you should also continue doing things that have a positive impact and work in your situation – until they no longer work.

For anyone that is struggling with parenting, regardless of how many children you have or if any have additional and complex needs, you are not alone. You are not the first parent struggling in the history of time, and you definitely won't be the last. Your own children will struggle at some point, too. I know I have made the same mistakes in some things as my mother did. I thought I knew better and then did it my way and it didn't work. I am sure my kids will also make similar mistakes. You can explain and give advice, but at the end of the day they will do what they think is best at the time. Continue what you are doing and trust yourself. If something doesn't work, try something new. Ask for help, get some rest, and no matter how badly the day seems to be going, it will end, and tomorrow will be a new day.

For anyone who interacts with a person with additional and complex needs – try and remember that they are trying their best, whether adult or child. They do not like the reactions they cause. They are not trying to be awkward and uncooperative. They are doing the best they can with whatever they are dealing with. An autistic person, for example, has different brain signals when they get anxious, and therefore may clap. That reaction is normal for them, not really any different from whatever reaction another person will have to their anxiety. No different to anyone with an issue. Imagine someone going through a divorce, or who may be stressed about other aspects of their life, say work or personal friendships. Everyone needs a little tolerance, so give them the benefit of the doubt. Maybe ask them if anything is wrong or if they want a chat over coffee.

I would love to hear any feedback, comments and suggestions for future publications. I have recently set up my own company towards helping those with additional and potentially extreme complex needs. I am also extremely passionate about inclusion, so I have combined both things in my company. This world contains so many different people and all of them can be amazing. If a company hired everyone the same, then it would not progress.

For anyone who is involved in employee resource groups over disabilities or inclusion, I would love to hear from you. Most employee resource groups generally have sub-groups which focus on some aspect of needs. In one company I worked for, they had numerous 'pillars', as they called them. They had an autism pillar, a pride pillar for LGBT, there was a pillar for mentoring women and ensure that the company recognised women for senior positions. Each pillar focused on a key area. Could any of this help your members? Is there anything I could do for your group or company? Communication is key to raising awareness for any condition and supporting all parties involved. I have given numerous talks about being autistic and being a carer to two children with their different conditions. I have spoken out about mental health, including the mental health issues I have suffered and recovered from. Language is the other key ingredient to develop awareness and change companies' perception of the employee with additional and complex needs.

Please feel to look at the website and subscribe for the latest information and details of lots of amazing things that are being done by charities. There are now such things as apps for autistic people, to help them self-manage their anxiety, and there is lots of information from councils and government about helping people who need that critical help – services which we can provide to help your company support you in the workplace, or help you support your family.

Contact:

Website: www.disabilityandinclusion.com
Email: information@disabilityandinclusion.com

Please subscribe and link to our social media accounts available on Facebook, Twitter and Instagram to keep updated with the latest articles, future publications or services.

ABOUT THE AUTHOR

Dave Russell was born and raised in South London. He now lives in Essex with his family and was diagnosed with autism in 2017. He has worked in the financial services industry for over ten years while raising awareness for disabilities in the workplace as well as support for those with dependants with disabilities. In the summer of 2018, he set up his own company which specialises in helping companies support their workforce from seminars, interactive discussions or awareness and educational material. He also works closely with schools creating educational material.

Printed in Great Britain
by Amazon

18133106R00109